HARCOURT HORIZONS

STATES AND REGIONS

D1552249

Assessment Program

SCHOOL PUBLISHERS

Orlando   Austin   New York   San Diego   Toronto   London

Visit *The Learning Site!*
www.harcourtschool.com

Printed in the United States of America

ISBN 10: 0-15-340287-3   ISBN 13: 978-0-15-340287-6

6 7 8 9 10 2266 20 19 18 17
4500687981

Contents

Overview

The assessment program in *Harcourt Horizons* allows all learners many opportunities to show what they know and can do. It provides you with ongoing information about each student's understanding of social studies.

The assessment program is designed around the Assessment Model in the chart below. The multi-dimensional framework is balanced between teacher-based and student-based assessments. The teacher-based strand typically involves assessments in which the teacher evaluates a student's work as evidence of his or her understanding of social studies content and ability to think critically about it. The teacher-based strand consists of two components: Formal Assessment and Performance Assessment.

The student-based strand involves assessments that invite the student to become a partner in the assessment process. These student-based assessments encourage students to reflect on and evaluate their own efforts. The student-based strand also consists of two components: Student Self-Evaluation and Portfolio Assessment.

The fifth component in the *Harcourt Horizons* assessment program is Informal Assessment. This essential component is shown in the center of the Assessment Model because it is the "glue" that binds together the other types of assessment.

ASSESSMENT MODEL
HARCOURT HORIZONS
Grades 3–6

Teacher-Based	Student-Based

Formal Assessment
• Lesson Reviews
• Chapter Reviews and Test Preparation
• Chapter Tests
• Unit Reviews and Test Preparation
• Unit Assessment
  Standard Tests
  Performance Tasks
	Student Self-Evaluation
	• Individual End-of-Project Summary
	• Group End-of-Project Checklist
	• Individual End-of-Unit Checklist

Informal Assessment • Review Questions • Social Studies Skills Checklist • Skills: Apply What You Learned	
Performance Assessment • Performance Activities • Unit Activities • Scoring Rubrics for Individual Projects • Scoring Rubrics for Group Projects • Scoring Rubrics for Presentations	**Portfolio Assessment** • Student-Selected Work Samples • Teacher-Selected Assessments • A Guide to My Social Studies Portfolio • Individual End-of-Unit Checklist • Social Studies Portfolio Summary • Portfolio Family Response

Description of Assessment Components and Materials in this Booklet

Informal Assessment

Informal Assessment is central to the Harcourt Horizons assessment program. Ultimately, it is your experienced eye that will provide the most comprehensive assessment of students' growth. This booklet provides a checklist to help you evaluate the social studies skills that your students demonstrate in the classroom (pages vi–vii).

Formal Assessment

This booklet provides Chapter and Unit Assessments (beginning on page 1) to help you reinforce and assess students' understanding of ideas that are developed during instruction. Each Unit Assessment includes standard tests and performance tasks. Answers to assessment items and suggested scores are provided in the Answer Key (beginning on page 117).

Student Self-Evaluation

Student self-evaluation encourages students to reflect on and monitor their own gains in social studies knowledge, development of group skills, and changes in attitude. In this booklet, you will find checklists for both individual and group self-evaluation (pages viii–x).

Performance Assessment

Social studies literacy involves more than just what students know. It is concerned with how they think and do things. This booklet provides scoring rubrics to help you evaluate individual projects, group projects, and student presentations (pages xi–xiii).

Portfolio Assessment

For portfolio assessment, students create their own portfolios, which may also contain a few required or teacher-selected papers. Included in this booklet are support materials to assist you and your students in developing portfolios and in using them to evaluate growth in social studies (pages xiv–xvi).

Social Studies Skills Checklist

Students' Names

Map and Globe Skills

understanding globes					
understanding the purposes and uses of maps					
comparing maps with globes					
understanding reference maps and thematic maps					
understanding map symbols					
understanding directional terms and finding direction					
understanding and measuring distance					
understanding and finding location					

Chart and Graph Skills

understanding and using picture graphs					
understanding and using charts and diagrams					
understanding and using bar graphs					
understanding and using calendars and time lines					
understanding and using tables					
understanding and using diagrams					
categorizing information in charts and graphs					

Reading Skills

locating and gathering information					
using context clues to understand vocabulary					
using illustrations/objects to understand vocabulary					
grouping and categorizing words					
understanding facts and main ideas					
identifying fact and opinion					
identifying cause and effect					
following sequence and chronology					
summarizing					
synthesizing					
making inferences and generalizations					
forming logical conclusions					
determining point of view					
evaluating and making judgments					
predicting likely outcomes					

(continued)

© Harcourt

Reading Skills (continued)					
understanding artifacts and documents					
understanding photographs and picture illustrations					
understanding fine art					
understanding safety and information symbols					
making observations					
asking questions					
expressing ideas in various ways					
writing and dictating					
speaking and listening					
dramatizing and role-playing simulations					
listing and ordering					
constructing and creating					
displaying, charting, and drawing					
using standard grammar, spelling, sentence structure, and punctuation					
using social studies terminology correctly					
identifying primary and secondary sources					
comparing and contrasting information					
drawing conclusions					
making predictions					
Citizenship Skills					
making thoughtful choices and decisions					
solving problems					
working with others					
resolving conflicts					
acting responsibly					
keeping informed					
respecting rules and laws					
participating in a group or community					
respecting people with differing points of view					
assuming leadership					
being willing to follow					
making decisions and solving problems in a group setting					
understanding patriotic and cultural symbols					

Name _____

Date _____

Individual Evaluation

Tell about and evaluate your project by completing these sentences.

1 My project was about _____

_____

2 These people helped me as I worked on my project: _____

_____

_____

3 I gathered information from these sources: _____

_____

_____

4 The most important thing I learned from doing this project is _____

_____

_____

5 I will use what I have learned to _____

_____

6 My evaluation of my project is _____

_____

I think I deserve this evaluation because _____

_____

7 I would like to say _____

_____

© Harcourt

Group
End-of-Project
Checklist

Group Evaluation

Mark the number that tells the score you think your group deserves.

How well did your group	High			Low
❶ plan for the activity?	4	3	2	1
❷ carry out group plans?	4	3	2	1
❸ listen to and show respect for each member?	4	3	2	1
❹ share the work?	4	3	2	1
❺ solve problems without the teacher's help?	4	3	2	1
❻ make use of available resources?	4	3	2	1
❼ record and organize information?	4	3	2	1
❽ communicate what was learned?	4	3	2	1
❾ demonstrate critical and creative thinking?	4	3	2	1
❿ set up for the activity and clean up afterward?	4	3	2	1

Write a short answer to each question.

⓫ What did your group do best? _____
_____
_____

⓬ What can you do to help your group do better work? ____
_____
_____

⓭ What did your group like best about the activity? _____
_____
_____

© Harcourt

Name _____ Date _____

Unit Title _____

In My Opinion

Decide whether you agree or disagree with each statement below. Circle the word that tells what you think. If you are not sure, circle the question mark. Use the back of the sheet for comments.

1. This unit was very interesting. **Agree ? Disagree**

2. I learned a lot. **Agree ? Disagree**

3. I enjoyed working in groups. **Agree ? Disagree**

4. I enjoyed working alone. **Agree ? Disagree**

5. I felt comfortable giving my ideas and raising questions. **Agree ? Disagree**

6. I was cooperative and helped others learn. **Agree ? Disagree**

7. I contributed my fair share to group work. **Agree ? Disagree**

8. I am getting better at making decisions and solving problems. **Agree ? Disagree**

9. I worked on social studies at home and in the community as well as at school. **Agree ? Disagree**

10. I understood the ideas in this unit. **Agree ? Disagree**

11. I think I am doing well in social studies. **Agree ? Disagree**

Write a short answer to each question.

12. What did you like best in this unit? Why?

   _____

13. What is something you can do better now than you could do before?

   _____

14. What is something you understand now that you did not understand

   before? _____

© Harcourt

Name _____

Date _____

Check the indicators that describe the student's performance on a project or task. The section with the most check marks indicates the student's overall score.

4 Point Score Indicators: The student
_____ gathers a lot of relevant, accurate information.
_____ shows thorough understanding of content.
_____ demonstrates strong social studies skills.
_____ exhibits outstanding insight/creativity.
_____ communicates ideas clearly and effectively.

3 Point Score Indicators: The student
_____ gathers sufficient relevant, accurate information.
_____ shows adequate understanding of content.
_____ demonstrates adequate social studies skills.
_____ exhibits reasonable insight/creativity.
_____ communicates most ideas clearly and effectively.

2 Point Score Indicators: The student
_____ gathers limited relevant, accurate information.
_____ shows partial understanding of content.
_____ demonstrates weak social studies skills.
_____ exhibits limited insight/creativity.
_____ communicates a few ideas clearly and effectively.

1 Point Score Indicators: The student
_____ fails to gather relevant, accurate information.
_____ shows little or no understanding of content.
_____ does not demonstrate social studies skills.
_____ does not exhibit insight/creativity.
_____ has difficulty communicating ideas clearly and effectively.

Overall score
for the project

Comments:

_____

© Harcourt

Note: Specific rubrics for scoring unit Performance Tasks are provided at point of use following the reduced performance task pages for each unit, which appear in the Teacher's Edition and at the back of this book.

Group Project Rubric

Check the indicators that describe a group's performance on a project or task. The section with the most check marks indicates the group's overall score.

4 Point Score Indicators: The group
_____ makes outstanding use of resources.
_____ shows thorough understanding of content.
_____ works very cooperatively; contributions are about equal.
_____ displays strong decision-making/problem-solving skills.
_____ exhibits outstanding insight/creativity.
_____ communicates ideas clearly and effectively.

3 Point Score Indicators: The group
_____ makes good use of resources.
_____ shows adequate understanding of content.
_____ works cooperatively; contributions are nearly equal.
_____ displays adequate decision-making/problem-solving skills.
_____ exhibits reasonable insight/creativity.
_____ communicates most ideas clearly and effectively.

2 Point Score Indicators: The group
_____ makes limited use of resources.
_____ shows partial understanding of content.
_____ works cooperatively at times, but contributions are unequal.
_____ displays weak decision-making/problem-solving skills.
_____ exhibits limited insight/creativity.
_____ communicates some ideas clearly and effectively.

1 Point Score Indicators: The group
_____ makes little or no use of resources.
_____ fails to show understanding of content.
_____ does not work cooperatively; some members don't contribute.
_____ does not display decision-making/problem-solving skills.
_____ does not exhibit insight/creativity.
_____ has difficulty communicating ideas clearly and effectively.

Overall score
for the project

_____

Comments:

Note: Specific rubrics for scoring unit Group Performance Tasks are provided at point of use following the reduced performance task pages for each unit, which appear in the Teacher's Edition and at the back of this book.

Name _____

Date _____

Check the indicators that describe the student's or group's presentation. The section with the most check marks indicates the overall score for the presentation.

4 Point Score Indicators: The presentation
_____ shows evidence of extensive research/reflection.
_____ demonstrates thorough understanding of content.
_____ is exceptionally clear and effective.
_____ exhibits outstanding insight/creativity.
_____ is of high interest to the audience.

3 Point Score Indicators: The presentation
_____ shows evidence of adequate research/reflection.
_____ demonstrates acceptable understanding of content.
_____ is, overall, clear and effective.
_____ shows reasonable insight/creativity.
_____ is of general interest to the audience.

2 Point Score Indicators: The presentation
_____ shows evidence of limited research/reflection.
_____ demonstrates partial understanding of content.
_____ is clear and effective in some parts but not in others.
_____ shows limited insight/creativity.
_____ is of some interest to the audience.

1 Point Score Indicators: The presentation
_____ shows little or no evidence of research/reflection.
_____ demonstrates poor understanding of content.
_____ is, for the most part, unclear and ineffective.
_____ does not show insight/creativity.
_____ is of little interest to the audience.

Overall score
for the project

_____

Comments:

Name _____

Date _____

A Guide to My Social Studies Portfolio

What Is in My Portfolio	Why I Chose It
1.	
2.	
3.	
4.	
5.	
6.	

I organized my portfolio this way because

_____

_____

© Harcourt

Name _____

Date _____

Goals	Evidence and Comments
1. Growth in understanding social studies concepts	_____ _____ _____
2. Growth in building social studies skills	_____ _____ _____
3. Growth in thinking critically and creatively	_____ _____ _____
4. Growth in developing democratic values and civic responsibility	_____ _____ _____

Summary of Portfolio Assessment

For This Review			Since Last Review		
Excellent	**Good**	**Fair**	**Improving**	**About the Same**	**Not as Good**

Date _____

Dear Family Members,

Here are samples of social studies work that your child and I have chosen for portfolio assessment. Please ask your child to explain what he or she has done. Then write a short note to your child in the space below, telling your thoughts about what you have seen. Please have your child bring the portfolio, with your note, back to school.

Sincerely,

_____

Dear _____

Family Member

_____

© Harcourt

Name _Elly Poland_   Date _____

1 Test

Part One: Test Your Understanding

MULTIPLE CHOICE

Directions **Circle the letter of the best answer.**

1 Which of the following describes the global address of the United States?
   A south of the equator
   B near the Indian Ocean
   C in North America
   D in the Eastern Hemisphere

2 Continents are—
   F low lands that lie along an ocean.
   G the largest land areas on Earth.
   H narrow pieces of land connecting two longer land areas.
   J imaginary lines that circle the globe.

3 What does relative location describe?
   A a place's exact location on Earth
   B the half of Earth where a place is located
   C the continent where a place is located
   D where a place is located in relation to other places

4 The Appalachian Mountains are located in which part of the United States?
   F the southern part
   G the western part
   H the eastern part
   J the northern part

5 What kind of land is found in the Great Basin?
   A land that is almost completely surrounded by water
   B flat land that rises above the surrounding land
   C mountains and valleys
   D dry, mostly desert land

6 A delta is formed when—
   F silt builds up at a river's mouth.
   G flowing water wears down the land.
   H silt builds up along riverbanks after floods.
   J people build levees along riverbanks.

(continued)

© Harcourt

Name _____ Date _____

7 Which of the following does *not* affect the climate of an area?
A the elevation of the land
B nearness to certain landforms or bodies of water
C distance from the equator
(D) the trees and plants that grow naturally on the land

8 Which of the following is *not* an example of extreme weather?
F tornadoes
G precipitation
H droughts
J hurricanes

9 Which of these is a fuel resource found in the United States?
(A) iron
B oil
C gold
(D) copper

10 When you recycle paper products, which natural resource are you helping to conserve?
F water
G coal
(H) trees
J minerals

MATCHING

Directions Match each term on the right with its meaning. Then write the correct letter in the space provided.

Meaning

11 _equator_ an imaginary line that circles the globe

12 _isthmus_ a narrow piece of land that connects two larger land areas

13 _elevation_ the height of the land

14 _mouth_ the place where a river empties into a larger body of water

15 _erosion_ the wearing away of Earth's surface

16 _precipitation_ water in the form of rain, sleet, or snow

17 _product_ something that people make or grow, usually to sell

Term

A. product
B. erosion
C. equator
D. isthmus
E. precipitation
F. mouth
G. elevation

(continued)

Name _____ Date _____

Part Two: Test Your Skills

USE LATITUDE AND LONGITUDE

Directions Use the map to answer the questions that follow.

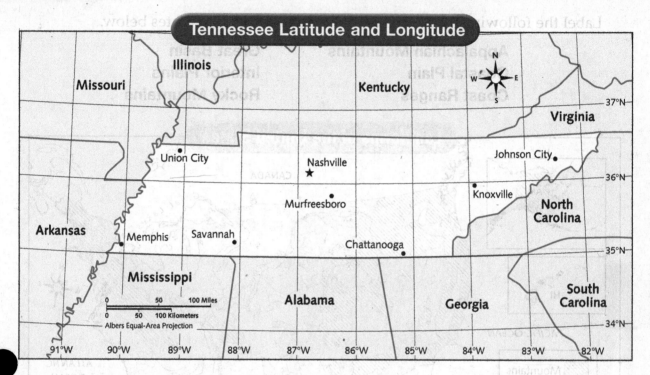

18 Between which two lines of
latitude does all of Tennessee lie? _____

19 What line of longitude is closest to
Union City, Tennessee? *89°w*

20 What city is located nearest
to 35°N, 90°W? *Memphis*

21 Which city is located near
36°N, 84°W? *Knoxville*

22 What lines of latitude and longitude
best describe the absolute location of
the capital of Tennessee? *36°N and 87°W*

(continued)

© Harcourt

Part Three: Apply What You Have Learned

Directions Complete each of the following activities.

23 **MAP LANDFORMS OF THE UNITED STATES**

Label the following landforms on the map of the United States below.

Appalachian Mountains	**Great Basin**
Coastal Plain	**Interior Plains**
Coast Ranges	**Rocky Mountains**

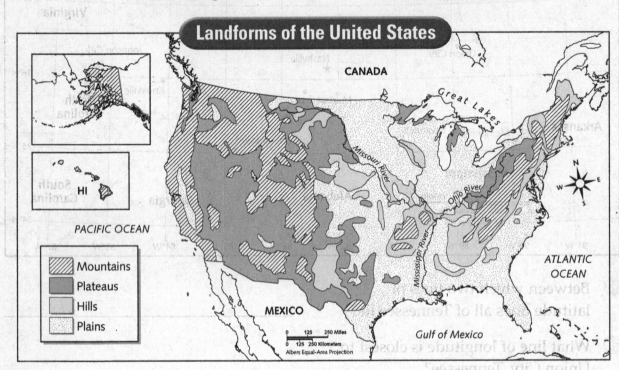

Landforms of the United States

24 **ESSAY**

In a one-paragraph essay, describe four kinds of natural resources found in the United States and explain why it is important to conserve those resources.

_____

_____

_____

_____

_____

2 Test

Part One: Test Your Understanding

MULTIPLE CHOICE

Directions Circle the letter of the best answer.

1 Why do people sometimes divide places into regions?
  A Regions make it easier to study and compare places.
  B Regions are necessary to find relative location.
  C Regions are important for helping the economy grow.
  D Regions help improve communication and trade.

2 Which of these best describes an urban region?
  F Stores and schools are often far away.
  G There are many houses instead of factories and tall buildings.
  H Most homes are built far apart.
  J The buildings are very tall and close together.

3 Which of these statements about counties is *not* correct?
  A A county has its own government.
  B A county is usually bigger than a state.
  C A sheriff enforces a county's laws.
  D A county is a political region.

4 Which of these is a region based on physical features?
  F the Rocky Mountains
  G oil-producing states
  H Medfield, Massachusetts
  J Chinatown, San Francisco

5 Which of these does *not* describe one type of economic region?
  A Many people there earn a living cutting down trees.
  B Many people there use the land for farming.
  C Many people there have the same religious beliefs.
  D Many people there have jobs making automobile parts.

6 A region based on a group's customs, foods, or language is—
  F an industrial region.
  G an urban region.
  H a mining region.
  J a cultural region.

(continued)

© Harcourt

7 Why may some physical regions change over time?

  A Groups of people move from place to place.

  B People build dams across rivers.

  C Businesses build factories nearby.

  D Farmers change the crops they grow.

8 People in different regions depend on one another because—

  F they share the same laws and government.

  G transportation connects different regions.

  H no one region has all the resources and products it needs.

  J some regions have no resources.

9 Which of the following is *not* a way that technology links people in different regions?

  A People are able to communicate with one another.

  B People are able to visit friends and family who live far away.

  C People are able to learn about what is happening in other regions.

  D People are able to walk to school, work, and stores.

TRUE OR FALSE

Directions Read each of the statements below. In the space next to each, write *T* if the statement is true. Write *F* if the statement is false.

10 _____ Many of the same kinds of regions found in the United States are found in other places around the world.

11 _____ A government is a system of deciding what kinds of jobs are best for a group of people.

12 _____ Physical regions have exact boundaries set by law.

13 _____ In service industries, workers are paid to do things for other people.

14 _____ Shaking hands when you meet someone is a custom.

15 _____ Much of the United States is covered by rain forest regions.

16 _____ People often modify the environment to meet their needs.

(continued)

Name _____   Date _____

Part Two: Test Your Skills

⚫ USE A LAND USE AND RESOURCE MAP

Directions Use the map of Montana to answer the questions that follow.

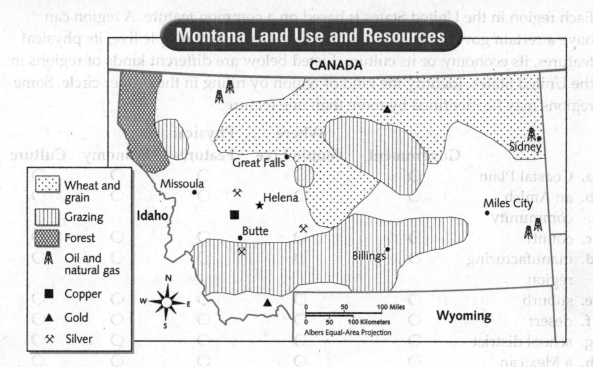

Montana Land Use and Resources

17 How is most of the land in
northeastern Montana used?   _____

18 Where are most of Montana's
forests located?   _____

19 What mineral resources are found
in Montana?   _____

20 Is the largest grazing area in northern
or southern Montana?   _____

21 What fuel resources are found near
Miles City, Montana?   _____

_____

(continued)

Part Three: Apply What You Have Learned

Directions Complete each of the following activities.

22 **CATEGORIZE THE KINDS OF REGIONS**

Each region in the United States is based on a common feature. A region can have a certain government, or it can be based on where people live, its physical features, its economy, or its culture. Listed below are different kinds of regions in the United States. Identify the kind of region by filling in the proper circle. Some regions may be identified by more than one feature.

	Government	Where People Live	Physical Features	Economy	Culture
a. Coastal Plain	○	○	○	○	○
b. an Amish community	○	○	○	○	○
c. county	○	○	○	○	○
d. manufacturing region	○	○	○	○	○
e. suburb	○	○	○	○	○
f. desert	○	○	○	○	○
g. school district	○	○	○	○	○
h. a Mexican American neighborhood	○	○	○	○	○
i. mining region	○	○	○	○	○
j. tourism region	○	○	○	○	○
k. Piedmont	○	○	○	○	○

23 **ESSAY**

Interdependence among different regions of the United States is possible partly because of the country's modern transportation system. In a one-paragraph essay, explain two ways that transportation helps connect people in the United States.

_____

_____

_____

_____

_____

_____

·UNIT·
1 Test

Part One: Test Your Understanding
MULTIPLE CHOICE

Directions Circle the letter of the best answer.

1 The global address of the United States includes which of the following hemispheres?
  A Northern and Western Hemispheres
  B Southern and Western Hemispheres
  C Northern and Eastern Hemispheres
  D Northern and Southern Hemispheres

2 What country forms much of the northern border of the United States?
  F Mexico
  G England
  H Spain
  J Canada

3 Which of the following is *not* an example of a landform?
  A valley
  B tributary
  C plain
  D mountain

4 Which of these mountain ranges is *not* located in the western United States?
  F Appalachian Mountains
  G Coast Ranges
  H Sierra Nevada
  J Cascade Range

5 The place where a river begins is called—
  A its channel.
  B its mouth.
  C its drainage basin.
  D its source.

6 Which of these statements best describes how a river erodes the land?
  F The river leaves silt at its mouth, forming a delta.
  G When the river's current slows down, it forms sandbars.
  H The river leaves silt on flood-plains after a flood.
  J The movement of water wears away Earth's surface.

(continued)

© Harcourt

7 The weather of a place over a long time is its—
A climate.
B humidity.
C precipitation.
D habitat.

8 How can an ocean affect climate?
F It can make a place cooler in summer and warmer in winter.
G It can make the air drier.
H It can make the winter longer.
J It can affect the amount of sunlight reaching a place.

9 Which of these is a way to conserve resources?
A removing insulation
B recycling products
C driving more often
D drinking bottled water

10 Which of these regions has an exact boundary and its own government?
F a city
G a county
H a state
J all of them.

11 Which of the following is a manufacturing job?
A sewing clothes
B cleaning houses
C cutting hair
D delivering mail

12 Which of the following is *not* a service job?
F repairing cars
G caring for sick people
H farming
J delivering mail

13 Why do people in different regions depend on one another?
A Each region needs resources and products from other regions.
B All regions have the same needs.
C Some regions have more money than other regions.
D Resources and goods are divided evenly among regions.

(continued)

COMPLETION

Directions Fill in the blank with the correct term from the list below. You will not use two terms.

channel	fuel	industry
mineral	mouth	peninsula
rural	technology	urban

14. Land that is almost completely surrounded by water is a _____.

15. The deepest part of a river or other body of water is called its _____.

16. People use metals from _____ resources to make wire, pots, pans, coins, and other products.

17. Most people in the United States live in _____ regions.

18. Many people in _____ regions earn their livings as farmers.

19. An _____ is all the businesses that make one kind of product or provide one kind of service.

20. Computers, fax machines, and telephones are examples of _____.

(continued)

Name _____ Date _____

SHORT ANSWER

Directions Write the answer to each question on the lines provided.

21 What are the highest and lowest points in North America, and where are they located?

_____

_____

_____

22 Why is fertile soil an important natural resource?

_____

_____

_____

23 Why do most people live in more than one region at the same time?

_____

_____

_____

24 What are some major industries in the United States?

_____

_____

_____

25 What are some forms of transportation in the United States?

_____

_____

_____

_____

Name _____ Date _____

Part Two: Test Your Skills

READ AN ELEVATION MAP

> **Directions** **Use the map below to answer the questions that follow.**

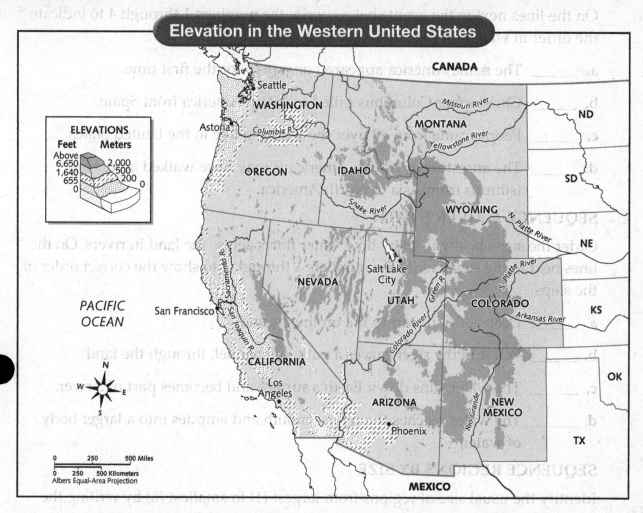

Elevation in the Western United States

26 What is the elevation of the land along most of the Pacific Coast? _____

27 Where in the western United States is the elevation of the land below sea level?

_____

28 What river's source is at a higher elevation, the Sacramento River's or the

Colorado River's? _____

29 Why do you think the elevation of the land in most of western Colorado,

Wyoming, and New Mexico is above 6,500 feet (2,000 m)? _____

_____

(continued)

© Harcourt

Part Three: Apply What You Have Learned

Directions Complete each of the following activities.

30 **SEQUENCE IMPORTANT EVENTS IN UNITED STATES HISTORY**

On the lines next to the events below, write the numbers 1 through 4 to indicate the order in which those events occurred.

a. _____ The name America appeared on a map for the first time.

b. _____ Christopher Columbus sailed to North America from Spain.

c. _____ People came from all over the world to live in the United States.

d. _____ The ancestors of Native Americans may have walked across an isthmus from Asia to North America.

31 **SEQUENCE A RIVER'S PATH**

Order the steps below to show how water flows across the land in rivers. On the lines next to the steps, write the numbers 1 through 4 to show the correct order of the steps.

a. _____ Drops of rain start to fall on the ground.

b. _____ Water in the river carves a path, or channel, through the land.

c. _____ The water runs down Earth's surface and becomes part of a river.

d. _____ The water reaches the river's mouth and empties into a larger body of water.

32 **SEQUENCE REGIONS BY SIZE**

Identify the usual size of regions from largest (1) to smallest (6) by writing the numbers 1 through 6 on the lines next to the regions below.

a. _____ country   **b.** _____ neighborhood

c. _____ county   **d.** _____ city

e. _____ state   **f.** _____ street

© Harcourt

(continued)

Name _____ Date _____

33 MAP REGIONS AROUND THE WORLD

Directions On the map below, each of Earth's oceans is labeled with a letter. Write the name of each ocean on the line beside its matching letter.

OCEANS

A. _____ B. _____

C. _____ D. _____

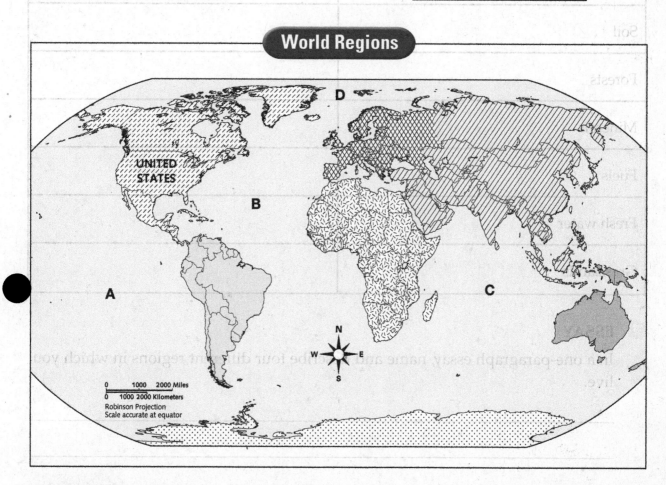

Directions Listed below are Earth's continents. Locate each continent on the map above and label it with the correct number.

CONTINENTS

1. Asia 2. Africa 3. North America
4. South America 5. Antarctica 6. Europe
7. Australia

(continued)

Unit 1 Test

Assessment Program ▪ 15

Name _____ Date _____ Date _____

34 CATEGORIZE NATURAL RESOURCES AND THE ECONOMY

Complete the table below by listing the kinds of jobs people in the United States might have that use each natural resource.

Natural Resource	Jobs
Salt water	
Soil	
Forests	
Minerals	
Fuels	
Fresh water	
Grasslands	

35 ESSAY

In a one-paragraph essay, name and describe four different regions in which you live.

_____

_____

_____

_____

Individual Performance Task

Landform Poems

In this task, you will use what you learned in Unit 1 to write and illustrate a haiku about the geography of the United States. A haiku is a short Japanese poem using words that do not rhyme. It often describes nature or someone's feelings about nature. A haiku has just three lines. The first line has five syllables, or parts of words. The second line has seven syllables, and the last line has five. Haikus usually do not capitalize the first letter of each line or use a period, comma, or other punctuation at the end of each line. For example:

> the United States   ← 5 syllables
> has many landforms, climates,   ← 7 syllables
> regions, and people   ← 5 syllables

1 Choose a landform that you read about in Unit 1 to be the subject of your haiku.

2 Write a first draft of your haiku. It should tell something about the landform—where it is located, its features, or why you chose it for your poem. You can use your textbook or library resources to write the haiku.

3 Review your haiku to be sure that it has the correct number of lines and the correct number of syllables in each line.

4 Illustrate your haiku with pictures from magazines or newspapers, or draw your own pictures.

5 Read your haiku to the class, and explain how your illustrations relate to the poem.

Name _____ Date _____

Group Performance Task

World Products

Interdependence means that people from different regions of the country and the world depend on one another for resources, products, and services. In this task, you will look in your home for products that come from other countries. Then you will work with a group to make a map and a list to show where these things came from. This activity will show that each person depends on people in other regions for many things.

1 Make a list of items in your home that come from other countries. Your list should include

- three pieces of clothing
- three food products
- three other kinds of manufactured goods

Your list should have the names of the products and the names of the countries from which they came. One list might include

- sneakers—Korea
- cookies—Canada
- T-shirt—Mexico
- television—Japan

2 Work with a small group of your classmates, and combine all the members' lists into a group list. Do not list the same item more than once.

3 Show all of your group's information on a poster. Find or draw three blank outline maps of the world. Paste them onto the poster, and label them "Clothing," "Foods," and "Other Manufactured Goods."

4 Use a color to shade in the countries from which your group's products came. Use a different color for each map. Make a map key for each map. In each map key, draw a symbol that represents each product. Place each map key symbol on the country where that product was made.

5 Present your poster to the class. Discuss with your classmates the kinds of things—from other countries—that all of you use. Listen as the other groups present their lists and maps. As a class, organize all the items in the lists by the continents from which they came. Discuss why certain items are likely to come from certain places around the world.

© Harcourt

Name _____ Date _____

3 Test

Part One: Test Your Understanding

MULTIPLE CHOICE

Directions Circle the letter of the best answer.

1 The explorer who named New England was—
A Christopher Columbus.
B John Smith.
C Samuel de Champlain.
D Amerigo Vespucci.

2 Which of the following is *not* a New England state?
F New Hampshire
G Connecticut
H Rhode Island
J New Jersey

3 Which of these natural resources did Native Americans in New England use to survive?
A silver and gold
B cattle and sheep
C granite and marble
D fish and berries

4 Why did the Pilgrims leave England and sail to North America?
F They were searching for gold.
G They wanted to practice their religion freely.
H They wanted to meet new people.
J They were searching for new trade opportunities.

5 Where were most of New England's earliest settlements built?
A along bays of the Atlantic Coast
B in the Connecticut River valley
C along the shores of Lake Champlain
D in the Green and White Mountains

6 Which of the following was *not* a major industry in colonial New England?
F agriculture
G shipping
H fishing
J mining

(continued)

7 Why were most early factories built along rivers?

A to use the power of the rushing water to run machines

B to be closer to the resources they used

C to be closer to their customers

D to provide drinking water for factory workers

8 Which of these makes up the largest part of New England's economy today?

F textile industries

G service industries

H shipping industries

J agricultural industries

9 What do citizens accomplish during town meetings?

A They determine the population of their town.

B They make important decisions about their town.

C They learn about other New England towns.

D They organize volunteers for town services.

IDENTIFICATION

Directions For each group of terms, circle the letter of the term that does *not* belong with the other two.

10 a. granite   b. colony   c. quarry

11 a. cape   b. harbor   c. common

12 a. industrial economy   b. sap   c. textile mill

13 a. recreation   b. specialize   c. fish farm

14 a. cranberries   b. potatoes   c. cotton

(continued)

Name _____ Date _____

Part Two: Test Your Skills

READ A TIME LINE

(Directions) **Use the time line at the bottom of this page to answer the following questions.**

⑮ What centuries are shown on this time line? _____

⑯ Into what equal time periods is this time line divided (from one white line to

the next)? _____

⑰ Why is 1774 an important year in Newfane's history? _____

_____

⑱ How many years was the railroad in operation in Newfane? _____

⑲ After what year would a visitor see electric lights in Newfane? _____

⑳ Which was built first, Newfane's Union Hall or Newfane's Moore Free Library?

_____

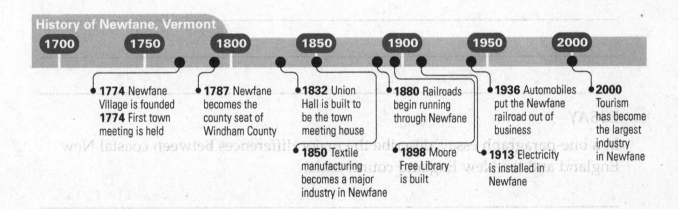

(continued)

Part Three: Apply What You Have Learned

Directions Complete each of the following activities.

21 CATEGORIZE PRODUCTS

List the products that people in New England produce using each of the following natural resources.

NATURAL RESOURCE	PRODUCTS
Trees	
Soil	

22 COMPARE AND CONTRAST TOWNS AND VILLAGES AROUND THE WORLD

List four things that these towns and villages have in common: Newfane, Vermont; Hawkshead, England; Tenterfield, Australia; St. Andrews, Canada.

_____

_____

_____

_____

_____

23 ESSAY

In a one-paragraph essay, describe the major differences between coastal New England and the New England countryside.

_____

_____

_____

_____

_____

Name _____ Date _____

4 Test

Part One: Test Your Understanding

MULTIPLE CHOICE

Directions Circle the letter of the best answer.

1 Henry Hudson was—
   A the leader of the Quakers.
   B one of the first Europeans to start a colony in North America.
   C one of the first Europeans to explore the Middle Atlantic region.
   D the person who named New York and New Jersey.

2 A loosely united group of governments working together is called a—
   F Society of Friends.
   G colony.
   H confederation.
   J treaty.

3 Which of the following is *not* a way that the Middle Atlantic Colonies were like the United States today?
   A The colonies welcomed people of all religions.
   B Farming was the largest part of the colonies' economy.
   C The largest cities were located along major waterways.
   D The colonies had a mix of people from different countries.

4 Which of the following is *not* a reason why the colonists decided to declare their independence from Britain?
   F The colonists had no representation in the British government.
   G New British laws made it difficult for the colonists to trade.
   H The British protected the colonists' trade and coasts.
   J New British laws forced the colonists to pay heavy taxes.

5 The Declaration of Independence states that—
   A Washington, D.C., would become the nation's capital.
   B all people have the right to life, liberty, and the pursuit of happiness.
   C all people should receive equal amounts of money.
   D Britain would give the colonists representation in their government.

(continued)

© Harcourt

6 Which of these port cities grew up on a harbor at the mouth of the Hudson River?

   F Philadelphia

   G Pittsburgh

   H Buffalo

   J New York City

7 The Erie Canal connected the Great Lakes to what body of water?

   A the Mississippi River

   B the Atlantic Ocean

   C the St. Lawrence River

   D the Pacific Ocean

8 Which of these resources is *not* needed to produce steel?

   F iron

   G oil

   H limestone

   J coal

9 Why did many immigrants move to Middle Atlantic cities during the late 1800s and early 1900s?

   A for low-cost housing

   B for factory jobs

   C to buy farmland

   D for service industry jobs

MATCHING

Directions **Match each term on the right with its meaning. Then write the correct letter in the space provided.**

Meaning

10 _____ a trading center where ships are loaded and unloaded

11 _____ deep and wide enough for ships to use

12 _____ the contest among companies to get the most customers or sell the most products

13 _____ a large city together with its suburbs

14 _____ to travel back and forth each day

Term

   A. commute

   B. competition

   C. metropolitan area

   D. navigable

   E. port

(continued)

© Harcourt

Name _____ Date _____

Part Two: Test Your Skills

IDENTIFY FACT AND OPINION

Directions Read the following statements about the Middle Atlantic region and decide whether they are facts or opinions. In the space next to each entry, write *F* if it is a statement of fact. Write *O* if it is a statement of opinion.

15. _____ New Amsterdam was the capital of the Dutch colony in the Middle Atlantic region.

16. _____ Religious freedom was the most important reason people settled in the Middle Atlantic Colonies.

17. _____ The Middle Atlantic Colonies were called the "breadbasket" colonies because they produced so much wheat.

18. _____ The Middle Atlantic Colonies were better than the New England Colonies.

19. _____ The Erie Canal helped trade grow in the Middle Atlantic region.

20. _____ The United States officially became an independent nation in 1783.

21. _____ An interstate highway is the most beautiful route for road travel.

22. _____ Steel was used to build railroad tracks, bridges, buildings, ships, and tools.

23. _____ New York City is the most exciting city in the United States.

24. _____ More people in the Middle Atlantic states live in cities than in rural areas.

(continued)

Part Three: Apply What You Have Learned

Directions Complete each of the following activities.

25 **SUMMARIZE TRANSPORTATION AND GROWTH**

In the space below, list four major forms of transportation that have helped the Middle Atlantic states grow and connect.

_____

_____

26 **SUMMARIZE THE PROBLEMS AND BENEFITS OF CITIES**

Though cities have much to offer, there are problems for people who live in them. List three benefits and three problems for people living in cities.

BENEFITS OF CITY LIVING	PROBLEMS OF CITY LIVING

27 **ESSAY**

In a one-paragraph essay, describe some of the actions that cities around the world have taken to solve urban problems.

_____

_____

_____

_____

_____

_____

_____

_____

_____

© Harcourt

Name _____ Date _____

2 Test

Part One: Test Your Understanding

MULTIPLE CHOICE

Directions Circle the letter of the best answer.

1 Why did the Pilgrims and Puritans settle in North America?

A because of the continent's many natural resources

B to start shipbuilding and fishing industries

C to trade with Native Americans for furs

D to practice their religions freely

2 A colony is—

F a settlement started by people who leave their country to live in another place.

G a point of land reaching out into the ocean.

H a person who comes to live in a country from some other place.

J a loosely united group of governments working together.

3 In an industrial economy—

A most people work along major rivers.

B people do not need farms and farmers.

C factories do not need raw materials.

D most goods are made in factories.

4 The first factory in the United States was built by Samuel Slater to produce—

F textiles.

G lumber.

H steel.

J flour.

5 The poor, rocky soil of New England is a result of—

A winds blowing the soil away.

B rivers eroding away the soil.

C glaciers moving across the land.

D inefficient farming methods.

6 Which of the following is *not* a way that the Middle Atlantic Colonies differed from the New England Colonies?

F People from many different countries came to live in the Middle Atlantic Colonies.

G The Middle Atlantic Colonies welcomed people of all religions.

H Much of the Middle Atlantic region has fertile soil.

J The Middle Atlantic Colonies had many busy ports.

(continued)

Name _____ Date _____

7 Why do some historians call Philadelphia the birthplace of the United States?
A The first colony was started there.
B The Declaration of Independence was signed there.
C The first fighting of the American Revolution took place there.
D It was the largest trading center in the American colonies.

8 When the United States first became a nation, what formed its western boundary?
F the Mississippi River
G the Atlantic Ocean
H the Appalachian Mountains
J the Great Lakes

9 Why did western Pennsylvania become a leading steel-producing region?
A It had a large population to supply workers for steel mills.
B It was surrounded by all of the natural resources needed to produce steel.
C It was linked to the Atlantic Ocean by the St. Lawrence Seaway.
D People used steel to build railroads, machines, and tall buildings.

10 Why are New York City, Philadelphia, and Boston important centers of trade?
F Many people work in these cities.
G They are all built on major waterways.
H They are all surrounded by large farming areas.
J They are all located along the Erie Canal.

11 Traffic, pollution, and trash in cities are all problems that are made worse by—
A climate.
B crowding.
C unemployment.
D tenements.

(continued)

Name _____ Date _____

MATCHING

> **Directions** Match each term on the right with its meaning. Then write the correct letter in the space provided.

Meaning	**Term**
⑫ _____ a place where ships can dock safely	A. quarry
⑬ _____ a large, open pit cut into the ground from which stone is mined	B. urban sprawl
⑭ _____ to work at only one kind of job and do it well	C. turnpike
	D. harbor
⑮ _____ in a river, a rocky place where a sudden drop in elevation causes fast-moving, dangerous water	E. specialize
⑯ _____ a road that drivers must pay to use	F. rapids
⑰ _____ the spreading of urban areas and the growth of new centers of business and shopping	

SHORT ANSWER

> **Directions** Write the answer to each question on the lines provided.

⑱ How did the Appalachian Mountains affect early water travel in the Northeast?

_____

_____

⑲ Why do steel mills in the Northeast no longer produce as much steel as they once did?

_____

_____

⑳ What kinds of jobs do many people have in cities in the Northeast?

_____

_____

(continued)

Part Two: Test Your Skills

USE A ROAD MAP AND MILEAGE TABLE

Directions Use the map and mileage table on page 31 to answer the following questions.

21 Which interstate highway connects Philadelphia, New York City, and Boston?

_____

22 How many miles separate Philadelphia and Pittsburgh, Pennsylvania? What highway could you take to travel from Philadelphia to Pittsburgh?

_____

23 How many miles is it from New York City to Dover?

_____

24 Which cities are farther apart, Boston and New York City or Pittsburgh and New York City?

_____

25 Which interstate highway follows the southern shore of Lake Erie?

_____

(continued)

© Harcourt

Name _____ Date _____ Date _____

Road Map of the Northeast

	Boston, MA	Dover, DE	New York City, NY	Philadelphia, PA	Pittsburgh, PA
NORTHEAST ROAD MILEAGE					
Boston, MA		378	206	296	561
Dover, DE	378		160	74	332
New York City, NY	206	160		91	368
Philadelphia, PA	296	74	91		288
Pittsburgh, PA	561	332	368	288	

© Harcourt

(continued)

Name _____   Date _____

Part Three: Apply What You Have Learned

Directions Complete each of the following activities.

26 **IDENTIFY CAUSES AND EFFECTS**

Complete the chart below to describe some of the causes and effects of changes and events that have occurred in the Northeast.

CAUSE	→	EFFECT
Huge glaciers moved across New England thousands of years ago.	→	_____ _____ _____
_____ _____ _____	→	The Middle Atlantic Colonies had a mix of people and cultures.
Many cities in the Northeast were built at the mouths of large rivers.	→	_____ _____ _____
_____ _____ _____	→	The United States became an independent nation.
People built the Erie Canal.	→	_____ _____ _____
Millions of immigrants moved to cities in the Northeast.	→	_____ _____ _____
_____ _____ _____	→	Western Pennsylvania became the center of the nation's steel industry.
Cities in the Northeast spread out and grew over time.	→	_____ _____ _____

(continued)

27 **IDENTIFY LOCATIONS ON A MAP**

Write the letters of the places listed below next to the numbers on the map to show the location of each place.

A. Albany, NY   **B.** Erie Canal   **C.** New York City

D. Appalachian Mountains   **E.** Hudson River   **F.** St. Lawrence Seaway

G. Buffalo, NY   **H.** Lake Erie   **I.** Atlantic Ocean

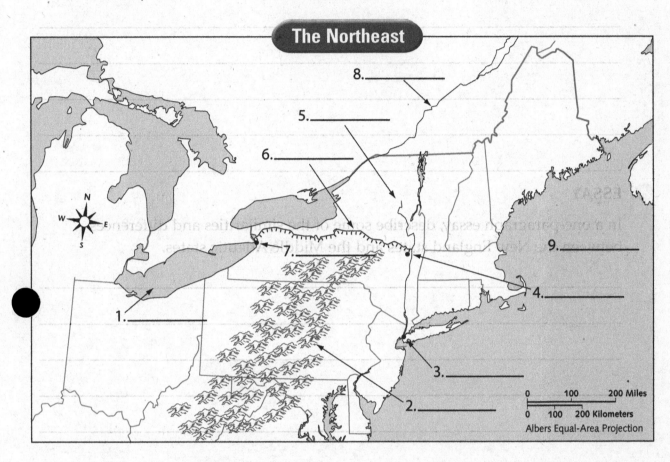

The Northeast

8. _____

5. _____

6. _____

7. _____

1. _____

9. _____

4. _____

3. _____

2. _____

0   100   200 Miles
0   100   200 Kilometers
Albers Equal-Area Projection

(continued)

© Harcourt

28 **MAKE GENERALIZATIONS ABOUT LIFE IN NEW ENGLAND**

List four ways people in New England have adapted to the region's cool climate and rocky soil in order to make a living.

_____

_____

_____

_____

_____

_____

29 **ESSAY**

In a one-paragraph essay, describe some of the similarities and differences between the New England states and the Middle Atlantic states.

_____

_____

_____

_____

_____

_____

_____

_____

© Harcourt

Individual Performance Task

And Now a Word About the Erie Canal

Your task is to write a newspaper advertisement for the newly opened Erie Canal. In your advertisement you are trying to get businesses to use the canal to ship their products. You can use facts from the box below to make your advertisement.

FACTS ABOUT THE ERIE CANAL

Length—363 miles
Width—42 miles
Depth—4 feet
Number of locks—83
Western end—Buffalo, New York
Middle—Syracuse, New York
Eastern end—Troy, New York
Nickname—"The Big Ditch"
Average speed for boats traveling on the Erie Canal—5 miles per hour
Time from Albany to Buffalo by horse—20 days
Time from Albany to Buffalo by canal—6 days

---

1 Gather information about the Erie Canal from your textbook and from other sources.

2 Write a first draft of your newspaper advertisement. Be creative, but make sure you are historically accurate.

3 Review your advertisement to be sure you have included all the important information. Draw a picture to illustrate your advertisement.

4 Have a classmate read your advertisement to see whether any part is unclear. If necessary, revise your advertisement.

5 Share the advertisement with your class, and then display it so that other students can read it.

© Harcourt

Group Performance Task

Town Meeting

The first recorded town meeting in New England was held in Dorchester, Massachusetts, in 1633. Since then, people in many New England towns have held town meetings to make important decisions. In this task, you will hold a mock town meeting to make decisions about your class.

1 With your small group, identify an issue or a problem you would like to present in the meeting. For example, you may wish to change the arrangement of the desks in the classroom. Or you may want to organize a canned-food drive for needy families, a homework support group, or a class party.

2 Gather information about your group's issue or problem, and write a short description of how you would like to address or solve it. For the issue of the desk arrangement, for instance, you may want to make a diagram of the present arrangement and another to show the way your group wants the desks to be rearranged. You may take a survey of your classmates to get their opinions about the issue. You could also speak to your teacher and principal.

3 As a class, hold your town meeting. Ask your teacher to conduct the meeting. One student from each group should be that group's representative, and the other students should take notes to record what happens in the meeting. Representatives should take turns presenting their issues to the class. Then the class should vote on the issue each representative presents.

4 Return to your group, and write a brief summary of what was decided in the meeting concerning your issue.

5 As a class, compile the group summaries into a class meeting announcement. Post your announcement outside your classroom. That way, students who did not attend the meeting can learn about the decisions that were made.

© Harcourt

Name _____ Date _____

5 Test

Part One: Test Your Understanding

MULTIPLE CHOICE

Directions Circle the letter of the best answer.

1 Where did Europeans first settle in the Atlantic Coast and Appalachian region?

A along the Mississippi River

B along the Coastal Plain

C on the Piedmont

D on the Cumberland Plateau

2 Why is Roanoke often called the "Lost Colony"?

F All of the first colonists of Roanoke died from starvation.

G No one knows why the first colonists of Roanoke disappeared.

H Roanoke Island is difficult to find on a map.

J The first Roanoke colonists lost all of their belongings in a hurricane.

3 To run machines, early settlers along the Fall Line used—

A waterpower.

B coal.

C natural gas.

D oil.

4 How did most early settlers cross the Appalachian Mountains to reach present-day Kentucky and Tennessee?

F by riding boats upriver from the Coastal Plain

G by walking or riding wagons through the Cumberland Gap

H by riding trains over the mountains

J by traveling up the Mississippi River from the Gulf of Mexico

5 In the past, why did many people in Appalachia make most of the things they needed?

A because craft products were popular items at festivals

B because they had few natural resources available

C because travel and trade were difficult in the mountains

D because they could not sell the products they made

(continued)

6 How did the Tennessee Valley Authority, or TVA, help the Atlantic Coast and Appalachian region grow?

F It built dams and power plants to supply water and electricity.

G It organized groups of settlers to move to the region.

H It cleared more land for farmers to plant crops in the region.

J It opened coal mines in the region, creating more jobs.

7 In which of the following states is coal mining a major industry?

A Maryland and Virginia

B Tennessee and North Carolina

C West Virginia and Kentucky

D Virginia and North Carolina

8 Which of the following is *not* a way in which government has helped some cities in the Atlantic Coast and Appalachian states grow?

F State capitals were located in some cities in the region.

G The national government is based in Washington, D.C.

H Government-owned high-tech industries are growing rapidly in the region.

J The government built some of the nation's largest military bases in the region.

MATCHING

Directions Match each term on the right with its meaning. Then write the correct letter in the space provided.

Meaning

9 _____ a place where rivers drop from higher to lower land

10 _____ a person who first settles a new place

11 _____ an opening between high mountains

12 _____ a lake that stores water held back by a dam

13 _____ a metal used to make things that need to be strong and light

14 _____ to return something, such as land, to its natural condition

15 _____ a place where people go to relax and have fun

16 _____ an area of land set aside to protect animals and other living things

Term

A. pass

B. resort

C. fall line

D. pioneer

E. reclaim

F. reservoir

G. wildlife refuge

H. aluminum

(continued)

© Harcourt

Name _____ Date _____

Part Two: Test Your Skills

READ A LINE GRAPH

Directions **Use the line graph to answer these questions.**

17 About how many people lived in
Virginia in 1850?

_____

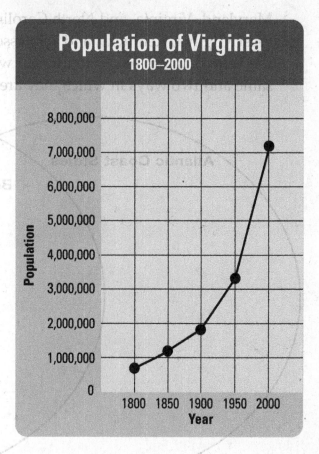

Population of Virginia
1800–2000

18 In which year was the population of
Virginia the highest? the lowest?

_____

19 In which 50-year period did the
greatest change in population
take place?

_____

20 What general statement can you
make about Virginia's population,
based on the line graph?

_____

_____

_____

21 Based on the line graph, what prediction can you make about the population of
Virginia in 2050?

_____

_____

_____

_____

(continued)

© Harcourt

Name _____   Date _____

Part Three: Apply What You Have Learned

Directions Complete each of the following activities.

22 **COMPARE AND CONTRAST INFORMATION**

Maryland, Virginia, and North Carolina are called the Atlantic Coast states, and West Virginia, Kentucky, and Tennessee are called the Appalachian states. Use the Venn diagram below to list four ways in which those state groups are the same and two ways in which they are different.

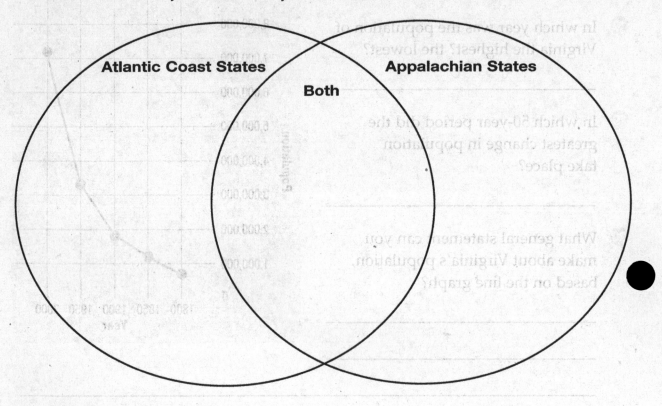

Atlantic Coast States   Appalachian States

Both

23 **ESSAY**

In a one-paragraph essay, explain why many cities in the Atlantic Coast and Appalachian states have grown up along rivers.

_____

_____

_____

_____

_____

_____

6 Test

Part One: Test Your Understanding

MULTIPLE CHOICE

Directions Circle the letter of the best answer.

1 Which state did Spanish explorer Ponce de León name in 1513?
A South Carolina
B Georgia
C Florida
D Alabama

2 How did early farmers use rivers in the Southeast and Gulf region?
F to irrigate their crops in the dry climate
G to ship their crops to markets
H to run mills to grind their wheat into flour
J to create hydroelectric power

3 Which of the following is *not* a way in which the North and South differed before the Civil War?
A More people in the North were moving to cities.
B More people in the North owned slaves.
C More people in the North wanted to abolish slavery.
D More people in the North worked in factories.

4 What effect did the Emancipation Proclamation eventually have?
F The American Civil War ended.
G Eleven Southern states seceded from the Union.
H All slaves in areas fighting the Union were given their freedom.
J Cotton plantations were made illegal in the South.

5 Which of these processed foods does *not* use a major crop grown in the Southeast and Gulf states?
A sugar
B peanut butter
C orange juice
D popcorn

(continued)

6 Which of these cities in the Southeast and Gulf states is *not* a port city?

  F Charleston, South Carolina

  G Atlanta, Georgia

  H Mobile, Alabama

  J Miami, Florida

7 Which of the following best describes the location of the Sun Belt?

  A in the southern part of the United States

  B in the northern part of the United States

  C along the Atlantic Coast of the United States

     along the Pacific Coast of the United States

8 Which of these islands or island groups is made of coral?

  F Hilton Head Island

  G Puerto Rico

  H the Florida Keys

  J the U.S. Virgin Islands

9 What do Brazil, India, and Greece all have in common with the Southeast and Gulf states?

  A tropical storms

  B coastal regions

  C fertile land

  D barrier islands

TRUE R FALSE

Directions Read each of the statements below about the Southeast and Gulf states. I the space next to each, write *T* if the statement is true. Write *F* if the statement s false.

10 _____ People from Spain were the first Europeans to explore the region.

11 _____ he region has a short growing season and plentiful rainfall.

12 _____ S e early farmers in the region started plantations.

13 _____ All f the Southeast and Gulf states were part of the Confederacy.

14 _____ The gion has few harbors or navigable rivers.

15 _____ Retire people make up a large part of the region's population.

16 _____ Hundre s of islands lie along the region's coasts.

17 _____ People u the region's forests to produce textiles.

(continued)

Name _____   Date _____

Part Two: Test Your Skills
COMPARE MAPS WITH DIFFERENT SCALES

Directions Study both maps below. Then answer the questions that follow.

18 About how many miles is it from Tampa to Orlando?

_____

19 About how many miles is it from Tallahassee to Lake City?

_____

20 Which map would you use to find the distance between Bradenton and Gainesville?

_____

_____

21 About how many miles is it from Melbourne to Ocala on Map A? on Map B?

_____

_____

22 Which map would you use if you needed information about both Jacksonville and Key West? Why?

_____

_____

(continued)

© Harcourt

Name _____   Date _____

Part Three: Apply What You Have Learned

Directions Complete each of the following activities.

23 CATEGORIZE SOUTHEAST AND GULF ISLANDS

Fill in the circle under the island or group of islands that fits each description. Sometimes more than one circle should be filled in.

	Barrier Islands	Puerto Rico	U.S. Virgin Islands	Florida Keys
a. protects the mainland during storms	○	○	○	○
b. People can drive to these islands.	○	○	○	○
c. Most food and water must be imported.	○	○	○	○
d. made of sand, shells, and soil	○	○	○	○
e. the peaks of underwater mountains	○	○	○	○
f. has rain forests and swamps	○	○	○	○
g. located in the tropics	○	○	○	○
h. popular with tourists	○	○	○	○
i. a territory of the United States	○	○	○	○
j. Residents are citizens of the United States.	○	○	○	○

24 ESSAY

In a one-paragraph essay, explain why the Southeast and Gulf region is a good location for farming.

_____

_____

_____

_____

_____

44 ■ Assessment Program   Chapter 6 Test

7 Test

Name _____ Date _____

Part One: Test Your Understanding

MULTIPLE CHOICE

Directions Circle the letter of the best answer.

1 Which of the following features is *not* found along the Gulf Coast of the South Central region?

A inlets

B beaches

C marshes

D deserts

2 Who were the first Europeans to claim land in the South Central region?

F the English

G the Spanish

H the French

J the Dutch

3 Why was Oklahoma settled by Europeans much later than the rest of the South Central states?

A The land was less fertile in Oklahoma.

B For many years, only Native Americans were allowed to live there.

C Oklahoma has no navigable rivers for transportation.

D The land in Oklahoma cost more than the land in other parts of the region.

4 How did Texas ranchers get their cattle to markets elsewhere in the country?

F They shipped the cattle on boats down rivers.

G They made the cattle walk the entire way.

H They shipped the cattle on railroads.

J They shipped the cattle on barges from the Gulf of Mexico.

5 What happens in a refinery?

A People build and test equipment for air and space travel.

B People use equipment to turn crude oil into useful products, such as gasoline.

C People dig out the bottoms and sides of waterways.

D People drill crude oil from the ground.

(continued)

6 Large ships can sail into the port of Houston, Texas, because—

F the city is located on the Atlantic Ocean.

G people built a canal linking the city to the Gulf of Mexico.

H people dredged the bayou, connecting the city to the Gulf of Mexico.

J the city is the nation's largest center for oil refining.

7 Which of these industries is *not* a major part of the South Central region's diverse economy?

A service industries

B drilling for oil

C farming and ranching

D coal mining

8 What caused a conflict between the United States and Mexico over their shared border?

F People disagreed about building dams on the Rio Grande.

G The channel of the Rio Grande moved south after floods.

H People in Texas used too much water for irrigation.

J Industries in Mexico were dumping harmful wastes into the Rio Grande.

9 Which of the following is *not* a way people in the United States and Mexico share the Rio Grande?

A They work together to build dams and reservoir projects along the river.

B They share the common border formed by the Rio Grande.

C They follow the same laws to prevent pollution in the river.

D They share the river's waters for irrigation.

IDENTIFICATION

Directions For each group of terms, circle the letter of the term that does *not* belong with the other two.

10 a. crude oil   b. aerospace   c. refinery

11 a. inlet   b. bayou   c. runoff

12 a. petrochemical   b. conflict   c. compromise

13 a. rid   b. expedition   c. irrigation

14 a. dredge   b. petroleum   c. wealth

15 a. El Chamizal   b. Rio Grande   c. Ozark Plateau

(continued)

Part Two: Test Your Skills

RESOLVE CONFLICTS

Directions Read each description of a conflict that has occurred in the South Central states. For each, describe the steps people took to resolve the conflict.

16 The Mexican government passed several laws raising taxes in Texas and limiting new settlement there. Many people in Texas thought these laws were unfair.

_____

_____

_____

_____

_____

17 People in Colorado, New Mexico, Texas, and Mexico all depend on the Rio Grande for irrigation. However, the riverbed was sometimes dry in parts of the Rio Grande valley.

_____

_____

_____

_____

_____

18 The channel of the Rio Grande moved south after floods. Land that had been part of Mexico was then north of the Rio Grande. People in the United States and Mexico disagreed about who owned that land.

_____

_____

_____

_____

_____

(continued)

© Harcourt

Name _____ Date _____

Part Three: Apply What You Have Learned

Directions Complete each of the following activities.

19 **CATEGORIZE FEATURES OF THE SOUTH CENTRAL STATES**

Use the graphic organizer below to describe the different ways the South Central states make up a region of variety. For each category, write three factors that illustrate the variety of the region.

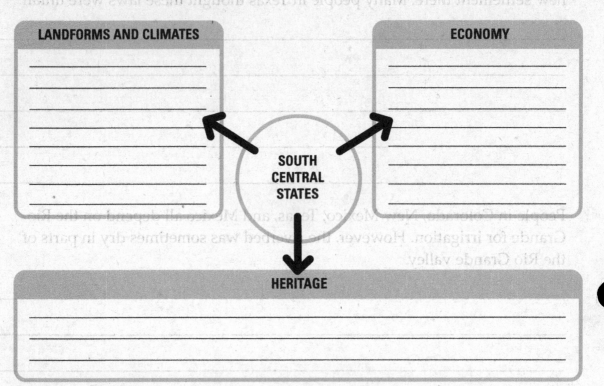

LANDFORMS AND CLIMATES

ECONOMY

SOUTH CENTRAL STATES

HERITAGE

20 **ESSAY**

Many industries in the South Central states depend on natural resources. In a one-paragraph essay, describe some of those industries and the natural resources they use.

_____

_____

_____

_____

_____

· U N I T ·

3 Test

Part One: Test Your Understanding

MULTIPLE CHOICE

Directions Circle the letter of the best answer.

1. What hardships did the early Jamestown colonists face?

   A Hurricanes blew in from the coast, destroying their homes.

   B They competed and fought with other colonists for land.

   C Much of the water they found was salty and unhealthy to drink.

   D They could not find any fertile soil to grow food.

2. Why did many cities along the Fall Line become centers of trade?

   F They were located along deep harbors on Chesapeake Bay.

   G Ships could go upstream from the Coastal Plain all the way to the Mississippi River.

   H The land around the Fall Line is good for farming.

   J They connected settlements along the Atlantic Ocean with the new settlements west of the Appalachian Mountains.

3. Which of the following is *not* a way people in the South region use rivers?

   A as transportation

   B to create electricity

   C for irrigation

   D to produce natural gas

4. Why do businesses often have offices in state capitals?

   F State laws require businesses to have offices in state capitals.

   G Businesses do not have to pay taxes in state capitals.

   H Business owners want to be near government leaders and offices that affect their work.

   J State capitals are always the largest cities in their states.

5. Why did most early Spanish expeditions come to explore the South region?

   A They came in search of religious freedom.

   B They came to drill for oil and natural gas.

   C They came in search of gold and other riches.

   D They came to start plantations.

(continued)

© Harcourt

6 How was the United States divided during the Civil War?
F into states that allowed slavery and states that did not allow slavery
G into the Confederacy, the Union, and border states
H into agricultural states and manufacturing states
J into territories claimed by the United States and territories claimed by France

7 Food processing and textile manufacturing are industries that—
A are related to agriculture.
B are located only along the Gulf Coast.
C need plentiful rainfall and a long growing season.
D rely on the South's nonrenewable resources.

8 Imports are—
F goods brought into one country from another country.
G trade among nations.
H goods shipped from one country to another country.
J resources that can be used to manufacture a product.

9 As you go from east to west across the South region—
A the elevation of the land gets lower.
B the cities get larger.
C the states get smaller.
D the climate becomes drier.

10 How are the South Central states different from the rest of the South states?
F They border the Gulf of Mexico.
G They have desert areas.
H They have several barrier islands off the coast.
J They do not have fertile land.

11 Which of the following events occurred first in the South region?
A English settlers started the Jamestown Colony.
B Spanish explorers claimed much of the region.
C The American Civil War was fought.
D The United States purchased the Mississippi River valley from France.

(continued)

TRUE OR FALSE

Directions Read each of the statements below about the South region. In the space next to each, write *T* if the statement is true. Write *F* if the statement is false.

12 _____ The region has many marshes, swamps, and bayous.

13 _____ Pioneers had to cross the Rocky Mountains to settle the entire region.

14 _____ Parts of the region were once claimed by Spain and France.

15 _____ All of the South states border either the Atlantic Ocean or the Gulf of Mexico.

16 _____ The region lies in the Sun Belt.

17 _____ None of the South states lie in the Interior Plains.

18 _____ The Mississippi River forms the western boundary of the South region.

19 _____ Tourism is a large industry in all of the South states.

SHORT ANSWER

Directions Write the answer to each question on the lines provided.

20 How did Daniel Boone help people settle parts of the South region?

_____

_____

_____

21 How do people in the South states use the region's forests to earn a living?

_____

_____

_____

22 Why is shipping a large industry in the South states?

_____

_____

_____

23 How did the discovery of oil affect parts of the South region?

_____

_____

(continued)

Part Two: Test Your Skills

COMPARE MAPS WITH DIFFERENT SCALES

Directions Study the two maps on page 53. Then use the maps to answer the following questions.

24 How are the two maps alike?

_____

25 How are the two maps different?

_____

_____

26 Look at the map scales on Map A and Map B. How many miles does one inch represent on each map?

_____

27 How many miles is it from Charleston to Myrtle Beach on Map A? on Map B?

_____

28 How many miles is it from Atlanta, Georgia, to Greenville, South Carolina? Which map did you use to answer this question?

_____

29 How many miles separate the capital of South Carolina and the capital of Georgia? Which map did you use to answer this question? Why?

_____

_____

30 If you were traveling to South Carolina on vacation, which map would you take with you? Why?

_____

_____

Map A: South Carolina

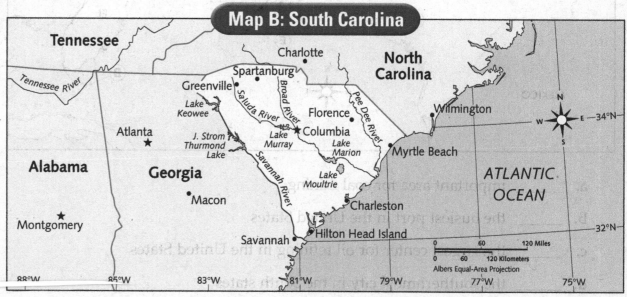

Map B: South Carolina

(continued)

Part Three: Apply What You Have Learned

Directions Complete each of the following activities.

31 **IDENTIFY LOCATIONS ON A MAP**

Match the description of each place below with the correct letter on the map.
Then write the letter in the space provided.

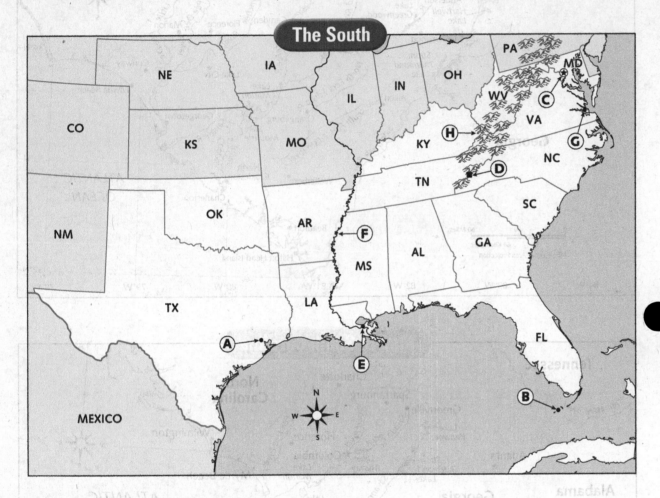

a. _____ important area for coal mining

b. _____ the busiest port in the United States

c. _____ the largest center for oil refining in the United States

d. _____ the southernmost city in the South states

e. _____ De Soto was among the first Europeans to cross this river

f. _____ the most-visited national park in the United States

g. _____ the center of the national government

h. _____ the first lasting English settlement in North America

(continued)

Name _____ Date _____

32 IDENTIFY CAUSE AND EFFECT

Complete the chart below to identify some of the causes and effects of changes and events that have occurred in the South.

CAUSE →	EFFECT
_____ _____ _____	Many cities in the South region are busy ports.
People from many different countries settled in the South region.	_____ _____
_____ _____ _____	Agriculture is an important industry throughout the South.
_____ _____ _____	The Rio Grande is the official border between the United States and Mexico.
People discovered large deposits of coal, oil, and natural gas in the South region.	_____ _____ _____

(continued)

© Harcourt

Name ______________________________ Date ______________

㉝ **IDENTIFY CAUSE AND EFFECT**

Listed below are three examples of decisions people have made in the South that changed the place where they lived. Describe two ways in which each of the decisions changed the environment of the South.

DECISIONS PEOPLE MADE	EFFECTS ON THE ENVIRONMENT
People decided to build coal mines in Appalachia.	
People decided to build dams and power plants in the Tennessee River Valley.	
People decided to develop tourism on the Florida Keys.	

㉞ **ESSAY**

The climate of the Sun Belt is generally mild all year long. In a one-paragraph essay, explain how this climate affects the South region.

Individual Performance Task

South Stamps

The first United States postage stamps were issued in 1847. Since then, the United States Postal Service has issued many special postage stamps called commemorative stamps. These stamps often honor people or events from the past that have had a great effect on the United States. Most commemorative stamps include an illustration, the name of the country that issued the stamp, and the value of the stamp. In some cases, the stamp's illustration also contains a brief title or description of what is pictured. If an event is shown, the stamp may also tell the date of the event.

1 Select one of the following topics for your postage stamp, or, with the approval of your teacher, select your own topic.

- The founding of the Jamestown Colony
- The Oklahoma land rush
- The Texas war for independence
- Crossing the Appalachian Mountains

- The American Civil War
- Islands of the South region
- Spanish exploration of the South
- The "Lost Colony" of Roanoke

2 Find information in your textbook and do research on the Internet or in your school's library to learn more about your topic.

3 Make a rough sketch of your stamp on a large sheet of paper. Make sure it contains all the parts of a real postage stamp.

4 Show your sketch to a classmate, and ask whether your design is clear and can be understood.

5 Improve the rough sketch and make any changes that are necessary.

6 Refer to your sketch to make a final copy of your stamp on posterboard.

7 Present and explain your postage stamp to the rest of the class. Then display your stamp in the classroom for others to enjoy.

Group Performance Task

Industry Report

Many of the major industries in the South have been an important part of the region's economy since colonial days. However, each of those industries has changed in many ways over time. In this task your group will create a presentation explaining the history of an industry in the South.

1 As a group, select one of the following industries to be the subject of your presentation, or, with the approval of your teacher, select your own topic.

- Agriculture
- Coal mining
- Oil production
- Tourism

- Cattle ranching
- Hydroelectric power
- Shipping and trade
- High-tech industries

---

2 Assign each member of your group a different aspect of the industry to research. Some aspects to consider are the history of the industry in the region; where in the region the industry is located today; and resources the industry uses.

3 Use your textbook, the Internet, and library resources to learn more about your topic. Each member of your group should try to find information that matches the aspect of the industry he or she is assigned.

4 As a group, make an outline of the information you will include in your presentation. Create illustrations, maps, graphs, or time lines to make the information easier to understand. You may also want to use photographs, artifacts, and quotations in your presentation.

5 Practice the presentation. Time yourselves with a watch to determine how long the presentation will take. It should be no longer than five minutes. All members of the group should prepare notes to help with their parts of the presentation.

6 Rehearse your presentation at least once. Be sure to use your illustrations, graphs, or other props in your rehearsal. Everyone in your group should give part of the presentation.

7 Give your industry presentation to the rest of the class. Then hold a short question-and-answer session about the industry.

Name _____ Date _____

8 Test

Part One: Test Your Understanding

MULTIPLE CHOICE

Directions Circle the letter of the best answer.

1 Why did Marquette and Joliet explore the Great Lakes region?
A to build trading posts along rivers
B to find and explore the Mississippi River
C to search for gold and silver
D to find a water route between Canada and the United States

2 Fighting over ownership of the Ohio River valley led to what war?
F the American Revolution
G the French and Indian War
H the American Civil War
J the War of 1812

3 Which of the following does **not** describe the Northwest Territory?
A It included the lands west of Pennsylvania and east of the Mississippi River.
B It was the first area in which the French built settlements in North America.
C It was divided into townships and sold to settlers.
D It included the lands north of the Ohio River and south of the Great Lakes.

4 Why did the United States decide to survey the Northwest Territory?
F to better plan for the settlement of the territory
G to set up a plan for governing the territory
H to describe the steps by which new states would be formed in the territory
J to plan where to locate capital cities in the territory

5 What caused the Great Lakes to form?
A glaciers
B floods
C earthquakes
D hurricanes

(continued)

© Harcourt

6 The Illinois Waterway and the Illinois River connect Lake Michigan with—
 F Lake Huron.
 G the Mississippi River.
 H Lake Superior.
 J the Ohio River.

7 Why were steel mills built along the Great Lakes?
 A The climate in the area is good for making steel.
 B No other region in the United States has coal.
 C Both iron ore and coal were found in nearby states.
 D There was a large automobile industry in the region.

8 Most manufactured goods today are—
 F made by hand.
 G made on assembly lines.
 H made by robots.
 J made in the Great Lakes states.

9 Which of these boats cannot travel upstream against a river's current?
 A flatboat
 B keelboat
 C steamboat
 D barge

COMPLETION

Directions **Fill in the blanks with terms from the list to complete the sentence. You will not use one term.**

10 In the Northwest Territory, one section in each

_____ was set aside for a school.

11 An _____ is a set of laws.

12 Settlers on the _____ were often surrounded by wilderness.

13 _____ is rock that contains one or more kinds of minerals.

14 The world's first _____ was built in Chicago in 1885.

15 Goods shipped on rivers are often called

_____ .

16 A _____ is a flat-bottomed boat used mostly on rivers and other inland waterways.

ore
frontier
skyscraper
ordinance
barge
paddy
township
freight

(continued)

© Harcourt

Name _____ Date _____

Part Two: Test Your Skills

MAKE A THOUGHTFUL DECISION

Directions **Read each decision people have made in the history of the Great Lakes states. For each, write one consequence of that decision.**

17 In 1673 French leaders in what is today Canada decided to send an expedition to explore the areas south of the Great Lakes.

_____

_____

_____

18 The United States government decided to sell land in the Northwest Territory for as little as a dollar per acre.

_____

_____

_____

19 Automobile manufacturers decided to use mass production in their factories.

_____

_____

_____

20 People decided to build locks and dams along the Mississippi River in the Great Lakes region.

_____

_____

_____

(continued)

Name _____ Date _____

Part Three: Apply What You Have Learned

Directions Complete each of the following activities.

21 **SUMMARIZE INFORMATION ABOUT RIVERS**

Complete the chart below to summarize information about some major rivers around the world.

RIVER	CONTINENT	USES
Mississippi River		
Nile River		
Chang Jiang		
Ganges River		
Amazon River		
Rhine River		

22 **ESSAY**

Mass production and the assembly line were two important developments in American industry. In a one-paragraph essay, explain what they are and why they are important.

_____

_____

_____

_____

_____

9 Test

Part One: Test Your Understanding

MULTIPLE CHOICE

Directions **Circle the letter of the best answer.**

1. Which of the following statements about the Plains region is *not* true?
   A The French were the first Europeans to explore the Plains region.
   B The Plains region includes both the Central Plains and the Great Plains.
   C Miles of prairie grasses once covered the Plains region.
   D Europeans settled in the Plains region before they settled in the Great Lakes region.

2. Why did the government pass the Homestead Act in 1862?
   F to encourage people to settle on the Great Plains
   G to set aside lands on the Great Plains for Native Americans
   H to encourage railroad companies to build tracks across the Great Plains
   J to clear more land for wheat farmers on the Great Plains

3. Why is prairie soil naturally very fertile?
   A There is little precipitation on the prairies.
   B When the prairie grasses die, they leave behind matter that enriches the soil.
   C Farmers add fertilizers to the soil.
   D When the Missouri River floods each year, it leaves behind rich silt.

4. What did most pioneers on the Great Plains use to build their homes?
   F sod
   G logs
   H buffalo skins
   J bricks

5. Where did many Sioux settle in the Plains region during the 1600s?
   A in Wisconsin and Minnesota
   B in Missouri and Iowa
   C in Kansas and Nebraska
   D in North Dakota and South Dakota

(continued)

© Harcourt

6 What crop changed farming on the Great Plains?

F dent corn

G sunflowers

H winter wheat

J rye grass

7 Why did meat packing become a major industry in the Plains states?

A because cattle and hogs are raised in the region

B because Texas ranchers drove their cattle to the Plains states

C because there is a low demand for meat in other regions

D because farmers in the region produce dent corn to feed the cattle

8 A fall in a demand for a good or service often leads to a fall in—

F temperature.

G supply.

H urbanization.

J free enterprise.

9 How are most of the world's plains used?

A for shipping

B for manufacturing

C for mining

D for agriculture

TRUE OR FALSE

Directions Read each of the following statements about the Plains states. In the space next to each, write *T* if the statement is true or *F* if the statement is false.

10 _____ All of the Plains states lie mostly in the Great Plains.

11 _____ The Sioux depended on buffalo for many of their needs.

12 _____ More people live on farms today than ever before.

13 _____ The Plains states, like all of the United States, have a free enterprise economy.

14 _____ For many years, corn and wheat were the two largest crops in the Plains region.

15 _____ Most early settlers in the Plains region had to be self-sufficient.

(continued)

© Harcourt

Name _____ Date _____

Part Two: Test Your Skills

● READ A DOUBLE-BAR GRAPH

[Directions] **The double-bar graph below shows the numbers of people living in urban and rural regions in each of the Plains states. Use the bar graph to answer the questions that follow.**

16 In which Plains states do more than 1 million people live in rural regions?

_____

_____

17 How do the urban and rural populations of Nebraska compare?

_____

_____

_____

_____

18 Do more people in the Plains states live in urban or rural regions?

_____

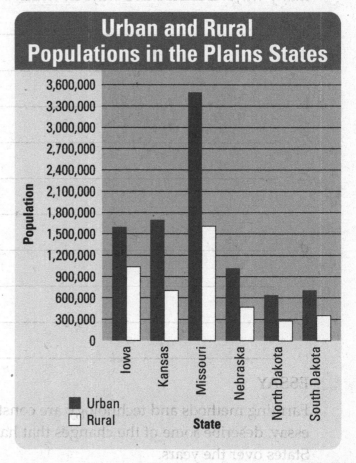

19 Which Plains state has the highest total population? How can you tell from this double-bar graph?

_____

_____

20 In which Plains state are the urban and rural population numbers closer, Kansas or South Dakota?

_____

(continued)

Name _____ Date _____

Part Three: Apply What You Have Learned

Directions Complete each of the following activities.

21 COMPARE PLAINS REGIONS

The Interior Plains in the United States and the Pampas in Argentina are alike in many ways. Describe five ways in which both areas are the same.

a. _____

_____

b. _____

_____

c. _____

_____

d. _____

_____

e. _____

_____

22 ESSAY

Farming methods and technology are constantly changing. In a one-paragraph essay, describe some of the changes that have affected farming in the United States over the years.

_____

_____

_____

_____

_____

_____

_____

© Harcourt

4 Test

Part One: Test Your Understanding

MULTIPLE CHOICE

Directions Circle the letter of the best answer.

1 Why are the six Great Lakes states grouped into one region?
 A because they are all major steel-producing states
 B because each of those states borders at least one of the Great Lakes
 C because the Great Lakes are the most important means of transportation for all of those states
 D because they are the only states in the United States that border the Great Lakes

2 One reason Detroit, Michigan, became a center for the automobile industry was that—
 F it was located in the center of the Middle West region.
 G there were many steel mills in Detroit to supply automobile manufacturers.
 H rivers and lakes made it easy to ship steel and automobiles in and out of Detroit.
 J the Mesabi Range, which holds large iron ore deposits, is located next to Detroit.

3 What made mass production of automobiles and other products possible?
 A navigable rivers
 B assembly lines
 C natural resources
 D hydroelectric power

4 Which of these is the longest river in the United States?
 F the Mississippi River
 G the Detroit River
 H the Ohio River
 J the Missouri River

5 What European country was the first to claim most of both the Great Lakes region and the Plains region?
 A Holland
 B England
 C Spain
 D France

(continued)

© Harcourt

6 When did the Plains region become part of the United States?

   F soon after the American Revolution ended in 1783

   G as part of the Louisiana Purchase of 1803

   H as part of the Homestead Act passed in 1862

   J as part of the Northwest Ordinance passed in 1787

7 Which of these is the main difference between the Central Plains and the Great Plains?

   A More people live on the Great Plains.

   B More corn is grown on the Great Plains.

   C The Central Plains get more precipitation.

   D The Central Plains are flatter and have fewer trees.

8 Which of these statements is *not* true of railroads in the Middle West?

   F They helped the ranching industry grow in the region.

   G Many cities grew up along their tracks.

   H They provided a way for settlers to move to the region.

   J They ended the need for the long Texas cattle drives.

9 Which of these storms is not likely to happen on the Interior Plains?

   A a blizzard

   B a tornado

   C a hurricane

   D a hailstorm

10 Which of the following is *not* a leading crop of the Middle West?

   F corn

   G wheat

   H peanuts

   J soybeans

11 Which of these is always true for plains regions?

   A Plains regions have fewer large cities than other regions.

   B Plains regions have mostly flat land.

   C Soil in plains regions is always fertile.

   D Cattle ranching is always a large industry on plains.

(continued)

© Harcourt

Part Two: Test Your Skills

READ A CULTURAL MAP

Directions As Europeans settled in the Americas over time, they brought their different cultures with them, including their languages. The cultural map on page 72 shows where in the Americas those languages are spoken today. Use the map to answer the following questions.

24 What language is spoken on most of the North American continent?

_____

25 What languages are spoken in Central America?

_____

26 What is the largest area of the Americas in which French is spoken?

_____

27 How does the map show you that people from Portugal settled parts of the eastern coast of South America?

_____

28 How does the map show you that Spain had settlements in both North America and South America?

_____

29 What on the map supports the idea that few Europeans settled in the inland areas of northern South America?

_____

_____

30 Which of the five European languages named in the map key is spoken least in the Americas today?

_____

(continued)

© Harcourt

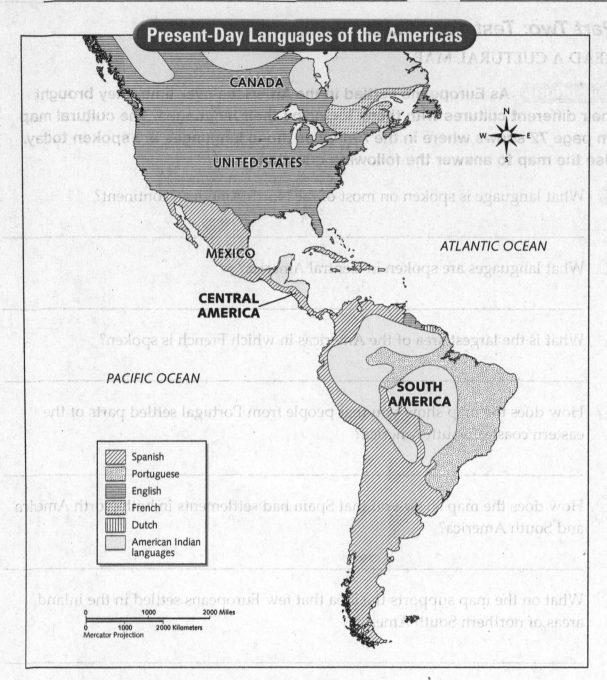

Present-Day Languages of the Americas

CANADA

UNITED STATES

ATLANTIC OCEAN

MEXICO

CENTRAL
AMERICA

PACIFIC OCEAN

SOUTH
AMERICA

Spanish
Portuguese
English
French
Dutch
American Indian
languages

0   1000   2000 Miles
0   1000   2000 Kilometers
Mercator Projection

(continued)

Part Three: Apply What You Have Learned

Directions Complete each of the following activities.

31 CATEGORIZE RESOURCES AND INDUSTRIES

For each resource or product of the Middle West in the table below, name an industry in that region that uses it.

RESOURCE OR PRODUCT	INDUSTRY
Wheat crops	
Cattle	
Steel	
Waterways	
Iron ore	

32 CATEGORIZE CITIES IN THE MIDDLE WEST

Many cities in the Middle West have grown up along waterways. For each city listed below, write *GL* if it grew up along the Great Lakes. Write *MS* if the city grew up along the Mississippi River system.

a. _____ Chicago, Illinois

b. _____ St. Louis, Missouri

c. _____ Cleveland, Ohio

d. _____ Milwaukee, Wisconsin

e. _____ Minneapolis, Minnesota

f. _____ Dubuque, Iowa

g. _____ Detroit, Michigan

h. _____ Kansas City, Kansas

(continued)

33 **DESCRIBE INTERDEPENDENCE IN THE MIDDLE WEST**

People who live in cities and on farms and ranches in the Middle West depend on one another. List three ways farmers and ranchers depend on city dwellers and three ways city dwellers depend on farmers and ranchers.

FARMERS AND RANCHERS DEPEND ON CITY DWELLERS	CITY DWELLERS DEPEND ON FARMERS AND RANCHERS

34 **SEQUENCE RIVER TRANSPORTATION**

In this unit you read about four types of river transportation in the United States—barges, flatboats, steamboats, and keelboats. In the chart below, place them in the correct order, from the first introduced to the last introduced.

FIRST   **LAST**

35 **ESSAY**

In a one-paragraph essay, describe how people have adapted to the environment of the Interior Plains over time.

_____

_____

_____

_____

_____

_____

_____

Individual Performance Task

Supplying Demands

Most businesses that succeed meet a demand, or supply something that many people are willing to pay for. In the Middle West region, for example, flour mills met the demand for grinding winter wheat, while Joseph McCoy's stockyard in Abilene, Kansas, supplied a way to ship cattle to eastern markets. In many ways, supply and demand are the secret to success in business. For this task you will imagine you are writing a plan for a business you want to start in your community.

1 Brainstorm ideas for your business. Think about the businesses that already exist in your community. Are there any products or services not available in your community that you think people would want, such as bicycle repairs, computer services, or party supplies? Consider your own interests, too, since you will most likely have to work long hours to start your business. Whatever you choose should be something you enjoy or care about.

2 Choose your business. Then use the Internet or library resources to gather information about that kind of business. Research similar businesses in your community or elsewhere. You may wish to conduct a survey in your community to ask people if your service or product is something people want.

3 Write a business plan describing what good or service you will supply and what demand it will meet. Explain why you think your business will be a success in your community. You may wish to add graphs, tables, maps, or illustrations to your plan to make the information clearer and more interesting.

4 Present your business plan to the class. Then ask their opinions about whether they think your business is a good idea for your community.

© Harcourt

Group Performance Task

Eyewitness News

In a television news story, a reporter usually talks to one or more people who have taken part in an event. Most news stories have an introduction, one or more interviews, and a conclusion. In this task, your group will imagine they are traveling back in time to cover a historical event. You will prepare a news story as though it will be broadcast on a television news program.

1. Select one of these topics for a news story or, with the approval of your teacher, select your own topic. Decide which role each member of your group will take.

TOPIC	ROLES
Life in a Sioux community in the 1700s	a reporter, a Sioux chief, a Great Plains settler, members of a Sioux family
Cattle ranching in the 1800s	a reporter, Joseph McCoy, a railroad worker, a cowhand on the cattle drives
The Dust Bowl	a reporter, a farmer on the Great Plains, a meteorologist, a soil erosion expert
The completion of Mount Rushmore	a reporter, one of the first visitors, a park ranger
The automobile industry along the Great Lakes	a reporter, Henry Ford, an automobile factory worker, a steel mill owner

2. Use your textbook and library resources to learn more about your topic. Each member of your group should try to find information that matches his or her role.

3. As a group, make an outline of the questions the reporter will ask and the answers that the others will give. Each person in the group should have specific things to say.

4. Practice the news story. Time yourselves with a watch to determine how long the story will take. It should be no longer than five minutes. All members of the group should prepare notes to help with their parts of the presentation.

5. Present the news story to the rest of the class. Everyone in the group should act as though they are on a live television program.

Name _____ Date _____

10 Test

Part One: Test Your Understanding

MULTIPLE CHOICE

Directions Circle the letter of the best answer.

1 Which of the following is *not* an area that Lewis and Clark explored?
A the Rocky Mountains
B the Great Plains
C the Pacific Coast
D the Mississippi Delta

2 The Continental Divide is—
F an imaginary line that circles Earth halfway between the North Pole and the South Pole.
G an imaginary line that runs north to south along the peaks of the Rocky Mountains.
H an imaginary line that divides Earth into the Eastern Hemisphere and the Western Hemisphere.
J an imaginary line that runs east to west across North America from the Atlantic Ocean to the Pacific Ocean.

3 Which of the following is the main reason the first Mormon settlers moved to the Mountain region?
A to mine gold and silver
B for the right to vote
C to start cattle ranches
D for religious freedom

4 In mountain regions, satellites have improved—
F transportation.
G international trade.
H weather conditions.
J communication.

5 Why do no trees grow above the timberline?
A because temperatures at that elevation are too cold for trees to grow
B because precipitation levels are too high at that elevation
C because forest fires spread quickly at that elevation
D because less sunlight reaches places at that elevation

© Harcourt

(continued)

6 Which of the following natural resources found in the Mountain states does *not* supply energy?
   F gold
   G coal
   H natural gas
   J uranium

7 How do most people earn a living in the Mountain states today?
   A in mining industries
   B in manufacturing industries
   C in service industries
   D in agricultural industries

8 Which of these mountain ranges has the highest mountain peak in the world?
   F the Alps
   G the Himalayas
   H the Andes
   J the Atlas

9 Trading one kind of good for another without using money is called—
   A importing
   B bartering.
   C irrigating.
   D exporting

MATCHING

Directions Match each term at the left with the location at the right that best relates to the term. Then write the correct letter in the space provided. One location will match more than one term.

Term	Location
10 _____ boomtown	A. South Pass
11 _____ wagon train	B. Yellowstone National Park
12 _____ suffrage	C. Denver, Colorado
13 _____ geyser	D. Andes Mountains
14 _____ public land	E. Wyoming
15 _____ terrace	

(continued)

© Harcourt

Part Two: Test Your Skills

READ A CUTAWAY DIAGRAM

Directions Use the cutaway diagram of an underground coal mine below to answer the questions that follow.

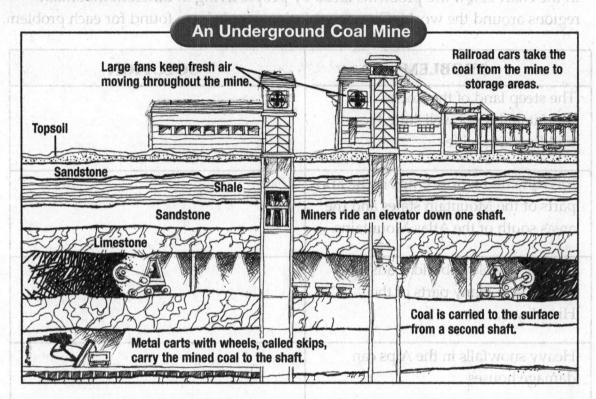

An Underground Coal Mine

- Large fans keep fresh air moving throughout the mine.
- Railroad cars take the coal from the mine to storage areas.
- Topsoil
- Sandstone
- Shale
- Sandstone
- Miners ride an elevator down one shaft.
- Limestone
- Coal is carried to the surface from a second shaft.
- Metal carts with wheels, called skips, carry the mined coal to the shaft.

16 What materials cover the coal buried underground?

_____

17 What keeps fresh air moving throughout the coal mine?

_____

18 How do miners get into the coal mine?

_____

19 How is the coal moved from the mine to storage areas?

_____

20 Why are there always two shafts in an underground coal mine?

_____

(continued)

© Harcourt

Name _____ Date _____

Part Three: Apply What You Have Learned

Directions Complete each of the following activities.

21 **SOLVE PROBLEMS**

In the chart below are problems faced by people living in different mountain regions around the world. Give one solution people have found for each problem.

PROBLEM	SOLUTION
The steep land of the Rocky Mountains is not well suited for building large cities.	
It is difficult to grow crops in the arid parts of the Mountain states and the areas south of the Atlas Mountains.	
It is impossible to build roads and railroads in many parts of the Himalayas.	
Heavy snowfalls in the Alps can damage houses.	
It is difficult to farm the steep land in the Andes Mountains.	

22 **ESSAY**

In a one-paragraph essay, describe how the Rocky Mountains have affected travel in the Mountain states over the years.

_____

_____

_____

_____

11 Test

Part One: Test Your Understanding

MULTIPLE CHOICE

Directions **Circle the letter of the best answer.**

1 Who led one of the first expeditions into the Southwest Desert region?
  A Meriwether Lewis and William Clark
  B Hernando de Soto
  C Francisco Vásquez de Coronado
  D Ponce de León

2 Which of the following physical features is *not* found in the Southwest Desert region?
  F canyons
  G mesas
  H coastal plains
  J deserts

3 What did the Anasazi use to build their homes?
  A wood
  B sod
  C buffalo skins
  D adobe

4 What city was built to be the capital of Spanish New Mexico?
  F Phoenix
  G Santa Fe
  H Las Vegas
  J Albuquerque

5 Why are natural sources of fresh water scarce in the Southwest Desert states?
  A because people use too much groundwater
  B because the region lies in the rain shadow of the western mountains
  C because most of the fresh water is used to irrigate farmland
  D because cloudbursts drop only small amounts of rain

6 Which of the following is *not* a way that people in the Southwest Desert states are working to conserve water resources?
  F creating water management areas
  G using rocks, sand, and desert plants in gardens
  H passing laws that forbid people from moving to the region
  J recycling water in artificial lakes and waterfalls

(continued)

© Harcourt

7 What features do all deserts have in common?

A a hot climate

B a dry climate

C sand dunes

D flat, level land

8 Which of these statements about oases is true?

F Most of the water at an oasis comes from underground springs.

G Irrigation is not possible in the loose sand at oases.

H An oasis is one of the driest places on Earth.

J Oases are formed by dams holding back water.

COMPLETION

Directions Fill in the blank with the correct term from the list to complete each sentence. You will not use every term.

9 A small steep hill of rock with a flat top is called a _____.

10 In a _____ early Spanish settlers taught Native Americans about Christianity.

11 On a _____ Native Americans govern themselves.

12 An _____ carries water from reservoirs to places where it is needed.

13 A _____ moves from farm to farm with the seasons, harvesting crops.

14 A _____ is formed as blowing sand forms hill-like mounds.

15 Negev farmers build plastic greenhouses over fields to prevent _____.

aqueduct

butte

evaporation

migrant worker

mission

nomad

reservation

sand dune

(continued)

Name _____ Date _____

Part Two: Test Your Skills

PREDICT A LIKELY OUTCOME

Directions **Predict the likely outcome in each case below based on the information given.**

16 About 1,000 years ago, the Anasazi began settling in Chaco Canyon in what is today New Mexico. They used irrigation to grow corn and other foods. During the 1100s, the Chaco Canyon area experienced decades of terrible droughts. What would have been the likely outcome for the Anasazi settlements there?

_____

_____

17 Spanish settlers from Mexico brought the first cattle into what is now the United States. Over time, some of those cattle wandered away, became wild, and spread across the region. Predict the effect this would have on the economy of the Southwest Desert states.

_____

_____

18 Over the years, many people from Mexico have immigrated to the Southwest Desert region. Predict how this might affect the cultural heritage of the Southwest Desert states.

_____

_____

19 People have built dams and reservoir projects in the Southwest Desert region to produce a steady supply of water and electricity. What effect might this have on

the population there? _____

_____

20 Many Southwest Desert states have passed laws against building new artificial lakes and waterfalls. They have also given awards to people who use rocks, sand, and desert plants in their gardens instead of grass. How do you think this will affect the Southwest Desert states in the future?

_____

(continued)

Part Three: Apply What You Have Learned

Directions Complete each of the following activities.

21 COMPARE DESERTS AROUND THE WORLD

Fill in the missing information in the table below to compare some major desert regions around the world.

DESERT REGION	LOCATION	HOW PEOPLE ADAPT TO THE DESERT ENVIRONMENT
Southwest Desert States		
Atacama Desert		
Sahara		
Negev		

22 ESSAY

As the population of the Southwest Desert states continues to grow, the region will need more and more water. In a one-paragraph essay, tell how people in the Southwest Desert states get water today.

_____

_____

_____

_____

_____

_____

© Harcourt

Name _____ Date _____

12 Test

Part One: Test Your Understanding

MULTIPLE CHOICE

Directions Circle the letter of the best answer.

1. Where did many of the first pioneers settle in the Pacific region?
   A in the Oregon Country
   B in Alaska
   C in the Sierra Nevada
   D in Death Valley

2. Boomtowns in the Pacific region often sprang up because of—
   F locations near important crossroads.
   G the discovery of gold.
   H dam and reservoir projects.
   J the discovery of oil.

3. What form of communication replaced the Pony Express?
   A telephones
   B computers
   C telegraphs
   D fax machines

4. Most of the labor on the first transcontinental railroad was done by—
   F Native Americans.
   G slaves.
   H immigrants.
   J miners.

5. Which of the following statements is *not* true of the Pacific region?
   A It has the top farming and manufacturing state in the United States.
   B It has the highest and lowest points in the United States.
   C It has the largest city and megalopolis in the United States.
   D It has the wettest and driest places in the United States.

6. What causes an earthquake?
   F A tropical storm forms off the Pacific Coast.
   G Hot gases, ash, and lava pour out from a crater.
   H The surrounding Pacific winds blow moisture over the land.
   J Layers of rock deep inside Earth move and crack.

(continued)

Name _____ Date _____

7 Which of these is an important industry in the Pacific Northwest?
A refining oil
B gold mining
C car manufacturing
D cutting lumber

8 Why do people live on only seven of the Hawaiian Islands?
F because transporting raw materials and finished products to and from the other islands is too expensive
G because the other islands have active volcanoes
H because the other islands are not important crossroads
J because the other islands are too small or windy, or have no fresh water

9 What is the smallest ocean in the world?
A the Arctic Ocean
B the Atlantic Ocean
C the Indian Ocean
D the Pacific Ocean

10 Which of the following is *not* true of most Pacific Rim countries?
F They all share the common border of the Pacific Ocean.
G They frequently experience earthquakes.
H They are all islands or groups of islands.
J They have many volcanoes.

MATCHING

Directions Match each term on the right with its meaning. Then write the correct letter in the space provided.

Meaning

11 _____ a gold seeker who arrived in California in the mid-1800s

12 _____ a narrow inlet of the ocean between cliffs

13 _____ the relationship between living things and the nonliving environment

14 _____ low-lying lands where the water level is always near or above the surface of the land

15 _____ a king or queen

16 _____ fresh fruits and vegetables

Term

A. ecosystem
B. forty-niner
C. fjord
D. monarch
E. produce
F. wetlands

(continued)

Part Two: Test Your Skills

● ACT AS A RESPONSIBLE CITIZEN

Directions For each topic below, list two ways that you could act as a responsible citizen.

17 Protecting the environment

_____

_____

_____

_____

18 Conserving natural resources

_____

_____

_____

_____

19 Helping people in your community

_____

_____

_____

_____

20 Learning about your community, state, and country

_____

_____

_____

_____

(continued)

Part Three: Apply What You Have Learned

Directions **Complete each of the following activities.**

㉑ COMPARE AND CONTRAST PACIFIC ISLANDS

Hawaii, Guam, and American Samoa are all located in the Pacific Ocean. Use the Venn diagram below to list two ways in which they are the same and one way in which they are different.

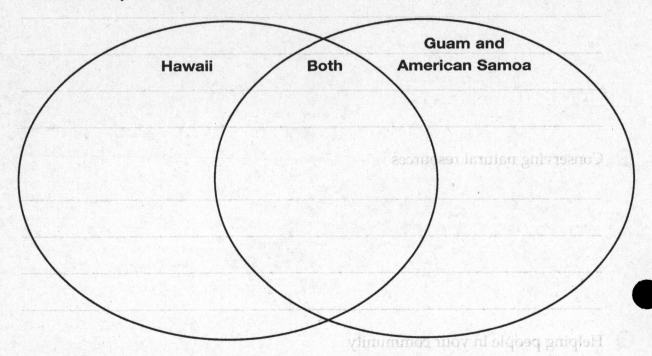

㉒ LIST PHYSICAL FEATURES

List six physical features that are found in the Pacific states.

_____

_____

_____

㉓ ESSAY

In a one-paragraph essay, describe how tourism plays an important role in the economy of the Pacific states.

_____

_____

_____

_____

Name _____ Date _____

·UNIT· 5 Test

Part One: Test Your Understanding

MULTIPLE CHOICE

Directions Circle the letter of the best answer.

1 Why are many peaks in the Rocky Mountains among the sharpest and highest in North America?
- A because the Rocky Mountains affect the flow of many rivers across the continent
- B because more snow falls on the peaks of the Rockies than at lower elevations
- C because erosion has not rounded or smoothed the peaks over time
- D because the Rocky Mountains are the oldest mountain range on the continent

2 The Rocky Mountains were a great barrier to east-to-west travel in the United States until—
- F the transcontinental railroad was built.
- G Lewis and Clark explored the mountains.
- H the first interstate highways were built.
- J airplanes were invented.

3 Which of these statements about temperature and mountains is true?
- A Mountain climates are always very cold.
- B Temperatures go down as you go up a mountain.
- C Warm temperatures stop trees from growing on mountains.
- D Mountain climates are always dry.

4 Which of these national parks is the oldest in the United States?
- F Grand Canyon National Park
- G Hawaii Volcanoes National Park
- H Yellowstone National Park
- J Petrified Forest National Park

5 What did the Hohokam and Anasazi Indians do that enabled them to live in one place?
- A They started using horses to hunt buffalo.
- B They won wars against their neighbors.
- C They discovered how to use adobe to build houses.
- D They developed irrigation systems to grow food.

(continued)

© Harcourt

6 Why do many people in the West region celebrate both Mexican and United States holidays?

    F Many families in the region trace their roots to Mexico.

    G People from Mexico were the first to live in the region.

    H Mexico was once part of the United States.

    J Both countries share the common border of the Rio Grande.

7 What effect do mountains have on the deserts in the West region?

    A The mountains prevent travel across the deserts.

    B When the mountain snows melt, they bring droughts to the deserts.

    C The mountains stop winds from creating sand dunes.

    D The mountains keep moist air from reaching the deserts.

8 What can cause a flood in the desert?

    F a cloudburst

    G a tornado

    H an arroyo

    J a drought

9 The climate of the Pacific Northwest is especially good for growing—

    A pineapples and coconuts.

    B cotton and wheat.

    C apples and pears.

    D oranges and grapefruit.

10 What were the last two states to join the United States?

    F Arizona and Nevada

    G Alaska and Hawaii

    H Oregon and Washington

    J Idaho and Montana

11 The nation's leading manufacturing state is—

    A Washington.

    B Arizona.

    C California.

    D Colorado.

12 Which of the following is *not* an industry in Hawaii?

    F banking

    G food processing

    H oil refining

    J tourism

(continued)

Name _____ Date _____

Date _____

MULTIPLE CHOICE

Directions For each group of terms, circle the letter of the term that does *not* belong with the other two.

13   **a.** Ring of Fire   **b.** Pacific Rim   **c.** Death Valley

14   **a.** fjord   **b.** mesa   **c.** butte

15   **a.** mission   **b.** oil slick   **c.** society

16   **a.** reservation   **b.** forty-niner   **c.** boomtown

17   **a.** sand dune   **b.** oasis   **c.** terrace

18   **a.** satellite   **b.** telegraph   **c.** geyser

19   **a.** rain shadow   **b.** migrant worker   **c.** barrier

SHORT ANSWER

Directions Write the answer to each question on the lines provided.

20   Where do most people in the western mountain regions live?

_____

_____

21   Why is water conservation especially important in the West region?

_____

_____

22   How did mining affect the West region?

_____

_____

23   How did the completion of the transcontinental railroad affect the West region?

_____

_____

(continued)

© Harcourt

Name _____ Date _____

Part Two: Test Your Skills

READ A TIME ZONE MAP

Directions Use the time zone map below to answer the questions that follow.

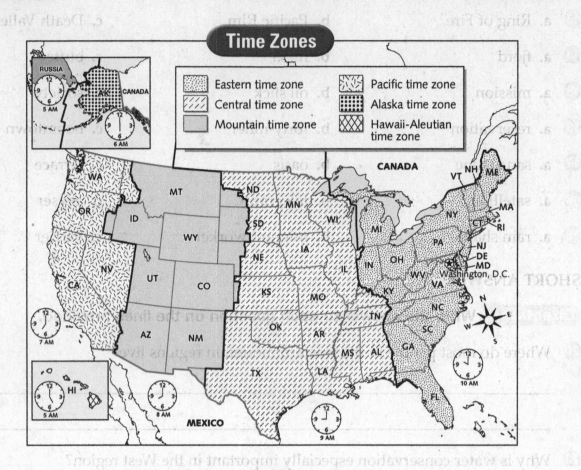

24 How many time zones are in the United States? _____

25 In which time zone is the capital of the United States located? _____

26 When it is 11:00 A.M. in Utah, what time is it in Iowa? _____

27 When it is 1:00 P.M. in Missouri, what time is it in California? _____

28 If you are in Nevada and you want to call a friend in Ohio when it is 9:30 P.M.

there, what time should you make the call? _____

Part Three: Apply What You Have Learned

Directions Complete each of the following activities.

29 **IDENTIFY WESTERN LOCATIONS ON A MAP**

Match each description below with the correct number on the map on page 94.
Write the number from the map in the space provided.

a. _____ the wettest place in the United States

b. _____ the city built to be the capital of Spanish New Mexico

c. _____ one of the only places in the United States with rain forests

d. _____ the lowest and driest place in the United States

e. _____ the highest mountain in the United States

f. _____ the place where the Anasazi settled

g. _____ the dam that created Lake Mead, one of the world's largest reservoirs

h. _____ the highest capital city in the United States

On the map on page 94, use a different color to shade each of the three regions of
the West—the Mountain states, the Southwest Desert states, and the Pacific states.
Then, in the chart below, fill in the names of the states that make up each region.

Mountain States	Southwest Desert States	Pacific States
_____	_____	_____
_____	_____	_____
_____	_____	_____
_____	_____	_____
_____	_____	_____

(continued)

The West

RUSSIA
AK ① CANADA
Bering Sea
0 250 500 Miles
0 250 500 Kilometers

CANADA

④ WA
OR
ID
MT
ND
MN
WI
SD
IA
WY
NE
NV
UT
CO ⑤
KS
MO
CA
③
⑧
⑦
AZ
⑥
NM
OK
AR

PACIFIC OCEAN

② HI
0 125 250 Miles
0 125 250 Kilometers

MEXICO

TX
LA

N
W   E
S

125 250 Miles
125 250 Kilometers
Albers Equal-Area Projection

Gulf of Mexico

Pacific States	Southwest Desert States	Mountain States

(continued)

© Harcourt

Name _____ Date _____

30 USE A TIME LINE

The time line below shows some important events that occurred in the West region during the past 200 years. Use the time line to answer the questions on page 96.

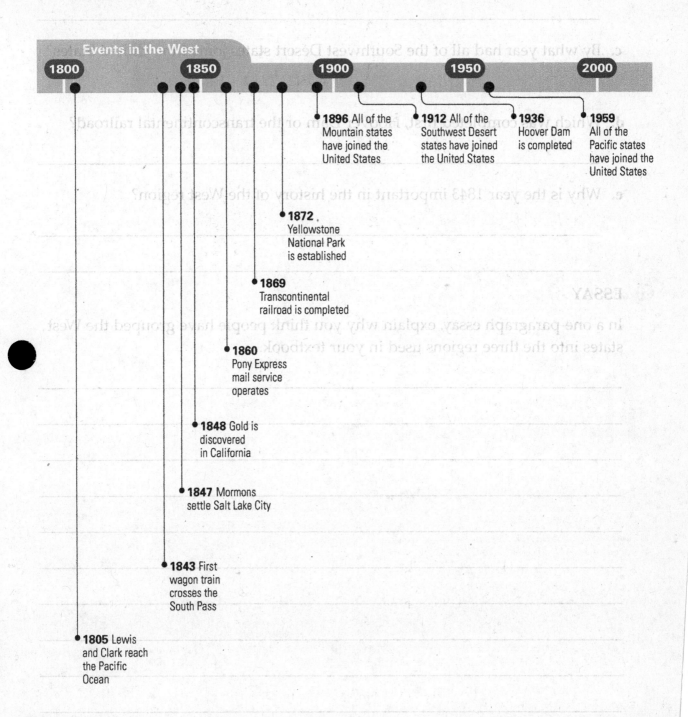

Events in the West

1800 1850 1900 1950 2000

1896 All of the Mountain states have joined the United States

1912 All of the Southwest Desert states have joined the United States

1936 Hoover Dam is completed

1959 All of the Pacific states have joined the United States

1872 Yellowstone National Park is established

1869 Transcontinental railroad is completed

1860 Pony Express mail service operates

1848 Gold is discovered in California

1847 Mormons settle Salt Lake City

1843 First wagon train crosses the South Pass

1805 Lewis and Clark reach the Pacific Ocean

© Harcourt

(continued)

a. When was Yellowstone National Park established?

_____

b. Which two events on the time line occurred within one year of each other?

_____

_____

c. By what year had all of the Southwest Desert states joined the United States?

_____

d. Which was completed first, Hoover Dam or the transcontinental railroad?

_____

e. Why is the year 1843 important in the history of the West region?

_____

_____

31 **ESSAY**

In a one-paragraph essay, explain why you think people have grouped the West states into the three regions used in your textbook.

_____

_____

_____

_____

_____

_____

_____

_____

_____

_____

_____

(continued)

Name _____ Date _____

Individual Performance Task

Western Environments

People throughout time have adapted to their different environments. In this task, you will write a short report on the ways in which a group of people adapted to their environment.

1 Select one of the following environments to analyze. Then select one of the groups that lives or lived in that environment to be the subject of your report.

DESERTS	MOUNTAINS	COASTS AND ISLANDS
Hohokam and Anasazi Indians	Sherpas	Nez Perce and Chinook Indians
Israelis	Quechuas	Hawaiians

2 Use your textbook, the Internet, or library resources to find out how your group adapted to the environment in which it lives or lived. Some of the things to consider are housing, farming, raising animals, industries, clothing, transportation, and culture.

3 Write a rough draft of your report. Have a classmate read it. Ask whether anything in the report is confusing.

4 Make a final copy of your report. Include with your final copy a map showing where your group lives or lived. You may also want to include pictures from magazines or newspapers, or draw your own pictures.

5 Share your report with your classmates.

© Harcourt

Unit 5 Test

Assessment Program ▪ 97

Group Performance Task

West Words

A *lexicon* is a collection of words. In this task, your small group will create a book called *A Lexicon of the West.*

1 With your group, brainstorm words from this unit, from *A* to *Z*, that deal with the West region of the United States. The words should be about the region's geography, economy, culture, or attractions. For example, an *A* word might be *adobe*, and a *B* word might be *boomtown*. The letter does not have to be the first letter of the word. For example, an *X* word might be *Phoenix*. Try to come up with as many words for each letter as possible.

2 As a group, choose one word for each letter of the alphabet. It should be one for which a picture could be drawn to show its meaning or importance.

3 Divide the letters of the alphabet among your group members. Each person should be responsible for about the same number of letters. Each student will create a page for the lexicon for each of his or her words. There should be three parts to each page.

➡ **PART 1**   At the top of the page will be a heading that gives the letter and the word, such as *A is for adobe* or *B is for boomtown.*

➡ **PART 2**   In the center of the page will be a drawing showing the meaning of the word. For example, *A is for adobe* could show a drawing of a pueblo.

➡ **PART 3**   At the bottom of the page will be a two-sentence explanation of the importance of the word. For example, you could write, "The Anasazi used adobe to build their homes in the Southwest Desert region. Today, many buildings in the region still use this style of architecture."

4 One student from the group should make a cover sheet for the lexicon. Another should make a Table of Contents. In the Table of Contents, there should be one line for each letter. It should state the name of the page, such as *A is for adobe*, and the name of the student responsible for the page. When the lexicon is finished, your group can display it for others to enjoy.

© Harcourt

Name _____ Date _____

13 Test

Part One: Test Your Understanding

MULTIPLE CHOICE

Directions Circle the letter of the best answer.

1 Which of the following is *not* one of the fastest-growing regions in the United States?

A the Sun Belt

B the Great Plains

C the Pacific Coast

D the Atlantic Coast

2 Which of the following statements explains why there are many different customs in the United States?

F There are many factories in the United States.

G The United States has a free enterprise economy.

H People from many places brought their customs here.

J As a country grows older, its people develop more customs.

3 Which of these do all people in the United States share?

A the same customs

B the same language

C the same government and laws

D the same foods and drinks

4 How do people in the United States remember their country's history?

F by celebrating holidays and visiting monuments

G by buying and selling goods and services

H by voting in general elections

J by volunteering in community organizations

5 In the United States, citizens do *not* have the right to—

A make choices about what kind of work to do.

B have a fair trial by jury.

C make decisions that take away the rights of others.

D say what they think about the government.

6 Which of the following is *not* a factor of production?

F human resources

G natural resources

H capital resources

J government resources

(continued)

7 If the demand for a good or service is high and the supply is low,—

A prices generally rise.

B prices generally fall.

C few people will want to buy it.

D the company will produce less of it.

8 Why do economic experts often call the time in which we live the "Information Age"?

F because the United States produces most of the movies in the world

G because more information and technology is available today than ever before

H because most Americans today work in high-tech industries

J because the United States takes part in the global economy

MATCHING

Directions **Match each term on the right with its meaning. Then write the correct letter in the space provided.**

Meaning	Term
9 _____ an unfair feeling of dislike or hatred for a group of people because of their background, race, or religion	A. monument
	B. democracy
10 _____ a saying chosen to express the ideals of a nation, state, or group	C. prejudice
11 _____ something that is built to remind people of the past	D. interest
12 _____ a form of government in which the people rule by making decisions themselves or by electing leaders to make decisions for them	E. majority rule
	F. motto
13 _____ a way of deciding something by voting	G. profit
14 _____ the money a business earns after everything is paid for	
15 _____ the money a bank or borrower pays for the use of money	

(continued)

© Harcourt

Name _____ Date _____

Part Two: Test Your Skills

DETERMINE POINTS OF VIEW

Directions Each of the state mottoes below was chosen to represent that state's ideals, people, geography, or history. Write a sentence or two explaining the point of view you think each state motto expresses.

16 **ALASKA:** "North to the Future"

_____

_____

_____

17 **INDIANA:** "The Crossroads of America"

_____

_____

_____

18 **KENTUCKY:** "United We Stand, Divided We Fall"

_____

_____

_____

19 **MASSACHUSETTS:** "By the Sword We Seek Peace, but Peace Only Under

Liberty" _____

_____

_____

20 **MICHIGAN:** "If You Seek a Pleasant Peninsula, Look Around You"

_____

_____

_____

_____

(continued)

Part Three: Apply What You Have Learned

Directions Complete each of the following activities.

21 IDENTIFY CAUSE AND EFFECT

Fill in the missing cause or effect to complete the chart below.

CAUSE	→	EFFECT
People in other countries sometimes face poverty and prejudice.	→	
	→	People in the United States eat oranges, apples, spaghetti, tacos, and egg rolls.
People in the United States volunteer to share responsibilities for the well-being of their communities.	→	
	→	People in the United States can live together in order and safety.
The United States takes part in the global economy.	→	

22 ESSAY

When President John F. Kennedy was a young man, he wrote a book about the United States. He called the book *A Nation of Immigrants*. In a one-paragraph essay, explain why this is a good title for a book about the history of the United States.

_____

_____

_____

_____

_____

© Harcourt

Name _____ Date _____

14 Test

Part One: Test Your Understanding

MULTIPLE CHOICE

Directions Circle the letter of the best answer.

1 Which of the following is *not* a purpose of the United States Constitution?

A to explain how our federal government works

B to unite the 50 states under one federal government

C to describe the rights that people in the United States have

D to organize the economy of the United States

2 In which branch of the federal government do senators work?

F the executive branch

G the military branch

H the legislative branch

J the judicial branch

3 How can the judicial branch of the federal government check the power of the legislative branch?

A by ruling that a law does not follow the Constitution

B by overriding a President's veto

C by rejecting a person chosen for the Supreme Court

D by vetoing a law passed by Congress

4 Which of the following is a responsibility of local governments?

F printing money

G delivering the mail

H building railroads

J collecting garbage

5 Why do all levels of government collect taxes?

A to conduct elections

B to ensure equal rights for all citizens

C to pay for the services they provide

D to pay for political campaigns

(continued)

© Harcourt

6 Which of the following rights is *not* guaranteed by the First Amendment to the United States Constitution?
  F freedom of religion
  G the right to vote in a general election
  H freedom of speech
  J the right to hold meetings to discuss problems and share information

7 Why does the United States form alliances with other countries?
  A to conquer these countries
  B to make sure everyone in the world follows the same religion
  C to maintain peaceful relations around the world
  D because it is required by the United Nations

CATEGORIZE

Directions Read each description below. If it describes the federal government, write *F* in the space. If it describes state governments, write *S* in the space. If the statement describes both levels of government, write *B* in the space.

8 _____ It collects taxes from citizens to pay for services.

9 _____ It prints and coins money in the United States.

10 _____ It oversees state colleges and state universities.

11 _____ It sets up court systems.

12 _____ It oversees trade with other countries.

13 _____ It provides for the public health and welfare.

14 _____ It sets up public schools.

15 _____ It declares war and makes peace.

(continued)

© Harcourt

Name _____ Date _____

Part Two: Test Your Skills

READ A FLOW CHART

Directions To make a law, state governments follow a process that is nearly identical to the process that the federal government follows. Fill in the missing information in this flow chart to explain how a bill becomes a law in the state governments.

HOW A BILL BECOMES A STATE LAW

A member of the state legislature introduces a _____.
16

↓

A _____ studies the bill and reports on it to the state legislature.
17

↓

Members of the _____ vote on the bill.
18

The governor

_____ **OR**
19
the bill.

The _____ **OR**
20
holds the bill and does nothing with it.

The governor

_____
21
the bill.

The bill becomes a

_____.
22

The bill returns to the state assembly

for a new _____.
23

At least two-thirds of the state legislature votes to override the governor's

_____.
24

(continued)

© Harcourt

Name _____ Date _____   Date _____

Part Three: Apply What You Have Learned

Directions Complete each of the following activities.

25 **COMPARE THE BRANCHES OF THE FEDERAL GOVERNMENT**

In the chart below, each box stands for a branch of the federal government.
Fill in the names of the three branches and the main job of each branch.

26 **ESSAY**

In 1863 President Abraham Lincoln gave a speech that came to be called the
Gettysburg Address. Read the following excerpt from that speech. Then write a
one-paragraph essay explaining what you think Lincoln was trying to express.

> "... our fathers brought forth on this continent, a new nation,
> conceived in Liberty, and dedicated to the proposition that all men
> are created equal. . . . we here highly resolve . . . that government
> of the people, by the people, for the people, shall not perish from
> the earth."

_____

_____

_____

_____

© Harcourt

Name _____ Date _____

6 Test

Part One: Test Your Understanding

MULTIPLE CHOICE

Directions Circle the letter of the best answer.

1 Why do some people call the United States a "nation of immigrants"?
- A The country has many visitors from around the world.
- B Most people in the United States are not citizens.
- C People from around the world have come here to live.
- D The country's economy is based on world trade.

2 Which of the following foods eaten in the United States did *not* come from other places?
- F corn
- G oranges
- H pasta
- J apples

3 What is the motto of the United States?
- A We the People
- B Out of Many, One
- C All for One, and One for All
- D Government of the People

4 Saluting the American flag during a parade expresses—
- F patriotism.
- G prejudice.
- H majority rule.
- J free enterprise.

5 Why is July 4 an important day for all Americans?
- A On that day, the American Civil War ended.
- B On that day, the United States declared independence from Britain.
- C On that day, the Pilgrims arrived in present-day Massachusetts.
- D On that day, representatives signed the United States Constitution.

6 In a democracy the people—
- F make choices about the government by voting.
- G are not represented in the government.
- H have few responsibilities.
- J have fewer rights than the leaders of the government.

(continued)

7 Which of the following is *not* a responsibility of citizenship?
   A voting in elections
   B obeying traffic signals
   C running campaigns
   D paying taxes

8 What do retail trade industries do?
   F loan, handle, and collect money
   G buy goods and sell them directly to consumers
   H produce and use information-processing software and hardware
   J buy large amounts of goods from producers and sell them to other businesses

9 What do most business owners consider when they decide what goods to produce or services to offer, and how much to charge for them?
   A supply and demand
   B the global economy
   C factors of production
   D interest on loans

10 What keeps any one branch of the government from becoming too powerful?
   F supply and demand
   G checks and balances
   H taxes and budgets
   J imports and exports

11 Which of these is a responsibility of the federal government?
   A fixing streetlights
   B selling farm products
   C running the army
   D collecting garbage

12 Which of these is a responsibility of a state government?
   F setting up public schools
   G buying fire trucks
   H delivering the mail
   J cleaning city streets

13 Which of the following is *not* a way that the Civil Rights movement worked to meet its goals?
   A holding demonstrations
   B organizing marches
   C not voting in elections
   D not buying certain products

(continued)

© Harcourt

⑭ MATCHING

Directions Match the terms on the left with the meanings on the right. Then, in the boxes on page 110, write each number next to the correct letter. You can check your work by adding the numbers in each row or column. You should get the same number as a sum no matter which row or column of numbers you add. Find this magic number.

Term	Meaning
a. immigrant	**1.** the document that gives the plan for the federal government
b. civil rights	**2.** the branch of the federal government that sees that the laws are carried out fairly
c. judicial branch	**3.** the condition of being poor
d. poverty	**4.** something that is built to remind people of the past
e. alliance	**5.** the head of the executive branch in state governments
f. governor	**6.** a signed request for action
g. county	**7.** the branch of government that makes the laws
h. capital resources	**8.** a partnership between countries or groups of people
i. majority rule	**9.** a form of government in which the people rule by making decisions themselves or by electing leaders to make decisions for them
j. democracy	**10.** the money, buildings, machines, and tools needed to run a business
k. legislative branch	**11.** the level of government for which a sheriff works
l. petition	**12.** a way of deciding something by voting
m. Constitution	**13.** a person who comes to live in a country from some other place
n. monument	**14.** a plan for spending money
o. budget	**15.** the branch of government that sees that laws that are passed are carried out
p. executive branch	**16.** the rights of citizens to equal treatment under the law

(continued)

© Harcourt

Name _____ Date _____ Date _____

Magic Number = _____

a. = _____	b. = _____	c. = _____	d. = _____
e. = _____	f. = _____	g. = _____	h. = _____
i. = _____	j. = _____	k. = _____	l. = _____
m. = _____	n. = _____	o. = _____	p. = _____

SHORT ANSWER

Directions **Write the answer to each question on the lines provided.**

15 Name two things that all people in the United States share and that help unite

them all. _____

_____

_____

16 How does the United States economy offer Americans choices?

_____

_____

_____

17 Why did early leaders of the United States add the Bill of Rights to the

Constitution? _____

_____

_____

18 Why does the United States play a special role among the countries of the world?

_____

_____

_____

(continued)

Name _____ Date _____

Part Two: Test Your Skills

READExample A POPULATION MAP

Directions Use the information in the population map on page 112 to answer the questions below.

19 Which part of the United States has a higher population density, the Atlantic Coast or the Pacific Coast? _____

20 In general, which country has a higher population density, Canada or the United States? _____

21 What is the population density in and around Mexico City, Mexico?

_____

22 Why do you think the area closest to the United States border has the highest population density in Canada? _____

_____

_____

23 Which part of Texas has a greater population density, the eastern half or the western half? Why do you think the population in Texas is spread out that way?

_____

_____

_____

24 Which city probably has more factories, Anchorage, Alaska, or Los Angeles, California? Explain your answer. _____

_____

_____

_____

(continued)

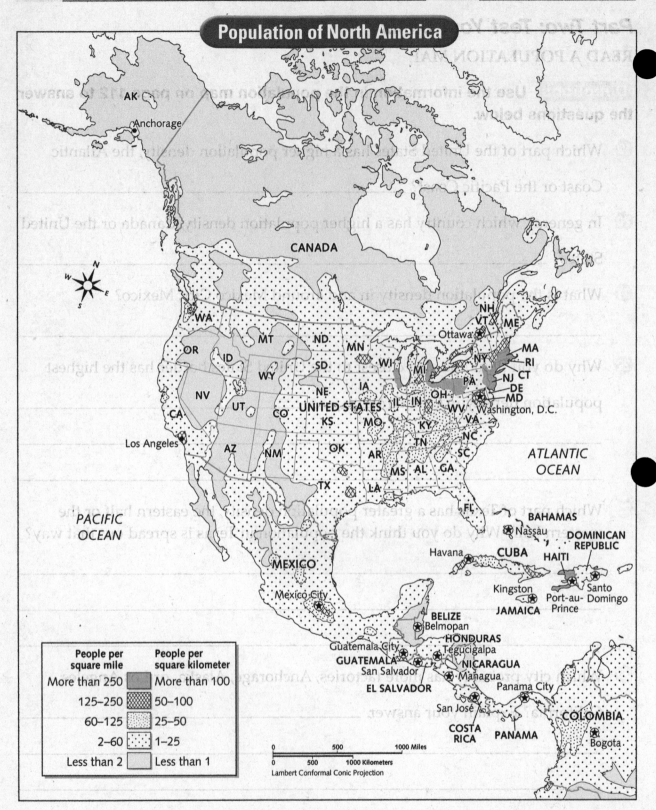

Population of North America

Legend:

People per square mile	People per square kilometer
More than 250	More than 100
125–250	50–100
60–125	25–50
2–60	1–25
Less than 2	Less than 1

Lambert Conformal Conic Projection

(continued)

Part Three: Apply What You Have Learned

Directions Complete each of the following activities.

25 **ANALYZE NATIONAL SYMBOLS**

Below are three symbols of our nation's heritage, history, and government. Explain what each symbol stands for.

_____

_____

_____

_____

_____

_____

_____

_____

_____

_____

_____

_____

_____

_____

(continued)

26 TRUE OR FALSE

Read each sentence below. Write *T* in the space next to the sentence if it is true and *F* if the sentence is false. If the sentence is false, cross out the word that makes it false and, above that word, write the correct word to make it true.

a. _____ In the past, most immigrants to the United States came from Europe.

b. _____ The United States government is a monarchy.

c. _____ The governor heads the executive branch of state government.

d. _____ Many immigrants came to the United States to escape wealth.

e. _____ State governments manage public utilities, such as water and electricity.

f. _____ When you vote on which game to play, you are using majority rule.

g. _____ During an election, most candidates carry on a petition.

h. _____ The United States takes part in the local economy by trading goods and services with other countries.

27 ESSAY

In a one-paragraph essay, describe how you think that your rights as a citizen of the United States relate to your responsibilities as a citizen.

_____

_____

_____

_____

_____

_____

_____

_____

Individual Performance Task

Immigrant Stories

As you know, immigrants from all over the world have been coming to the United States for centuries. They have come in search of a new life in a new place with new opportunities. In this task, you will create the diary of a young immigrant who has come to America with his or her family.

① Select one of the following stories as the basis for your diary:

- an immigrant coming to the American colonies for religious freedom
- an immigrant coming to the United States in the late 1800s or early 1900s to escape poverty
- an immigrant coming to the United States today to escape wars in his or her homeland

② Use a blank outline map of the world to show the country from which you have come, where in the United States you have settled, and the route you took to get to the United States.

③ Use your textbook, library resources, and the Internet to research the country from which you came and the region of the United States where you have settled.

④ Write at least five diary entries for different events that occurred during your immigration to the United States. One of the entries should explain why you left your home country. Another entry should tell about an experience you had on your journey and describe the mode of transportation you used. A third entry should describe how you felt when you reached your new home. The remaining entries should tell about events and experiences of your daily life as a newly arrived immigrant in the United States. Be creative, but be historically accurate as well.

⑤ Use pictures from newspapers or magazines to illustrate some of your diary entries, or draw your own pictures. Write a caption for each picture to describe what it shows and to identify which diary entry it is illustrating.

⑥ Make a cover for your diary, and share your diary with your classmates.

© Harcourt

Group Performance Task

City Council Election

The city council is an important part of local government. It makes the laws for its city, just as state legislatures and Congress make the laws for states and the nation. In this task, your class will hold a mock election for members of your city council.

1 **Select Candidates** In this election, six members will be elected to the city council. Form groups of three students each. One student in each group will be the candidate for city council, one will be the campaign manager, and one will be the campaign worker.

2 **Select Issues** As a class, choose five major issues in your community to be the platform of the campaign. Perhaps you can invite a member of your city council to speak to the class about some of the major issues in your community. Newspapers and your local library are sources where you can get information about local issues.

3 **Organize a Campaign** Decide among your group what position your candidate will take on each issue. Make up campaign posters to tell people about your candidate. You may wish to use a catchy slogan, or saying, on the posters. The campaign manager and worker should make flyers that tell what the candidate believes. They should hand out the flyers to other students.

4 **Give Campaign Speeches** Each campaign manager will give a one-minute speech introducing the candidate to the class. Each candidate will then give a two-minute speech to the class, explaining his or her ideas and positions on the issues.

5 **Go to the Polls** Using a secret ballot, each student—including the candidates—should vote for six members of the city council. Announce the results of the election. Then discuss how individual campaigns might have led to the success of certain candidates.

© Harcourt

Answer Key

ANSWERS

Name _____ Date _____

1 Test

Part One: Test Your Understanding

MULTIPLE CHOICE (3 points each)

Directions Circle the letter of the best answer.

1 Which of the following describes the global address of the United States?
A south of the equator
B near the Indian Ocean
C in North America
D in the Eastern Hemisphere

2 Continents are—
F low lands that lie along an ocean.
G the largest land areas on Earth.
H narrow pieces of land connecting two longer land areas.
J imaginary lines that circle the globe.

3 What does relative location describe?
A a place's exact location on Earth
B the half of Earth where a place is located
C the continent where a place is located
D where a place is located in relation to other places

4 The Appalachian Mountains are located in which part of the United States?
F the southern part
G the western part
H the eastern part
J the northern part

5 What kind of land is found in the Great Basin?
A land that is almost completely surrounded by water
B flat land that rises above the surrounding land
C mountains and valleys
D dry, mostly desert land

6 A delta is formed when—
F silt builds up at a river's mouth.
G flowing water wears down the land.
H silt builds up along riverbanks after floods.
J people build levees along riverbanks.

Name _____ Date _____

7 Which of the following does *not* affect the climate of an area?
A the elevation of the land
B nearness to certain landforms or bodies of water
C distance from the equator
D the trees and plants that grow naturally on the land

8 Which of the following is *not* an example of extreme weather?
F tornadoes
G precipitation
H droughts
J hurricanes

9 Which of these is a fuel resource found in the United States?
A iron
B oil
C gold
D copper

10 When you recycle paper products, which natural resource are you helping to conserve?
F water
G coal
H trees
J minerals

MATCHING (4 points each)

Directions Match each term on the right with its meaning. Then write the correct letter in the space provided.

Meaning		Term
11 __C__ an imaginary line that circles the globe		A. product
12 __D__ a narrow piece of land that connects two larger land areas		B. erosion
13 __G__ the height of the land		C. equator
14 __F__ the place where a river empties into a larger body of water		D. isthmus
15 __B__ the wearing away of Earth's surface		E. precipitation
16 __E__ water in the form of rain, sleet, or snow		F. mouth
17 __A__ something that people make or grow, usually to sell		G. elevation

(continued)

Chapter 1 Test

Assessment Program ▪ 1

2 ▪ Assessment Program

Chapter 1 Test

(continued)

Name _____ Date _____

Part Two: Test Your Skills

USE LATITUDE AND LONGITUDE (4 points each)

Directions Use the map to answer the questions that follow.

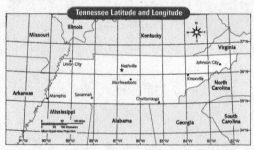

Tennessee Latitude and Longitude

18 Between which two lines of latitude does all of Tennessee lie? _____ 35°N and 37°N

19 What line of longitude is closest to Union City, Tennessee? _____ 89°W

20 What city is located nearest to 35°N, 90°W? _____ Memphis, TN

21 Which city is located near 36°N, 84°W? _____ Knoxville, TN

22 What lines of latitude and longitude best describe the absolute location of the capital of Tennessee? _____ 36°N, 87°W

(continued)

Chapter 1 Test

Assessment Program ▪ 3

Name _____ Date _____

Part Three: Apply What You Have Learned

Directions Complete each of the following activities.

23 MAP LANDFORMS OF THE UNITED STATES (12 points)

Label the following landforms on the map of the United States below.

Appalachian Mountains   Great Basin
Coastal Plain   Interior Plains
Coast Ranges   Rocky Mountains

Landforms of the United States

24 ESSAY (10 points)

In a one-paragraph essay, describe four kinds of natural resources found in the United States and explain why it is important to conserve those resources.

Possible response: Natural resources in the United States include soil, forests, water, minerals, and fuels. People depend on these resources to grow or make the things they need or want. However, all natural resources are limited, and some can never be replaced once they are used up. So it is important for people to protect natural resources and use them wisely.

© Harcourt

4 ▪ Assessment Program

Chapter 1 Test

ANSWERS

Name _____ Date _____

2 Test

Part One: Test Your Understanding

MULTIPLE CHOICE (3 points each)

Directions Circle the letter of the best answer.

1 Why do people sometimes divide places into regions?
(A) Regions make it easier to study and compare places.
B Regions are necessary to find relative location.
C Regions are important for helping the economy grow.
D Regions help improve communication and trade.

2 Which of these best describes an urban region?
F Stores and schools are often far away.
G There are many houses instead of factories and tall buildings.
H Most homes are built far apart.
(J) The buildings are very tall and close together.

3 Which of these statements about counties is *not* correct?
A A county has its own government.
(B) A county is usually bigger than a state.
C A sheriff enforces a county's laws.
D A county is a political region.

4 Which of these is a region based on physical features?
(F) the Rocky Mountains
G oil-producing states
H Medfield, Massachusetts
J Chinatown, San Francisco

5 Which of these does *not* describe one type of economic region?
A Many people there earn a living cutting down trees.
B Many people there use the land for farming.
(C) Many people there have the same religious beliefs.
D Many people there have jobs making automobile parts.

6 A region based on a group's customs, foods, or language is—
F an industrial region.
G an urban region.
H a mining region.
(J) a cultural region.

Chapter 2 Test   *(continued)*   Assessment Program ■ 5

Name _____ Date _____

7 Why may some physical regions change over time?
A Groups of people move from place to place.
(B) People build dams across rivers.
C Businesses build factories nearby.
D Farmers change the crops they grow.

8 People in different regions depend on one another because—
F they share the same laws and government.
G transportation connects different regions.
(H) no one region has all the resources and products it needs.
J some regions have no resources.

9 Which of the following is *not* a way that technology links people in different regions?
A People are able to communicate with one another.
B People are able to visit friends and family who live far away.
C People are able to learn about what is happening in other regions.
(D) People are able to walk to school, work, and stores.

TRUE OR FALSE (3 points each)

Directions Read each of the statements below. In the space next to each, write *T* if the statement is true. Write *F* if the statement is false.

10 __T__ Many of the same kinds of regions found in the United States are found in other places around the world.

11 __F__ A government is a system of deciding what kinds of jobs are best for a group of people.

12 __F__ Physical regions have exact boundaries set by law.

13 __T__ In service industries, workers are paid to do things for other people.

14 __T__ Shaking hands when you meet someone is a custom.

15 __F__ Much of the United States is covered by rain forest regions.

16 __T__ People often modify the environment to meet their needs.

6 ■ Assessment Program   *(continued)*   Chapter 2 Test

Name _____ Date _____

Part Two: Test Your Skills

USE A LAND USE AND RESOURCE MAP (4 points each)

Directions Use the map of Montana to answer the questions that follow.

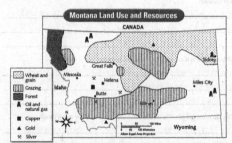

Montana Land Use and Resources

17 How is most of the land in northeastern Montana used? _____ for wheat and grain farming

18 Where are most of Montana's forests located? _____ in the northwestern part of the state

19 What mineral resources are found in Montana? _____ gold, copper, and silver

20 Is the largest grazing area in northern or southern Montana? _____ in southern Montana

21 What fuel resources are found near Miles City, Montana? _____ oil and natural gas

Chapter 2 Test   *(continued)*   Assessment Program ■ 7

Name _____ Date _____

Part Three: Apply What You Have Learned

Directions Complete each of the following activities.

22 **CATEGORIZE THE KINDS OF REGIONS** (22 points)

Each region in the United States is based on a common feature. A region can have a certain government, or it can be based on where people live, its physical features, its economy, or its culture. Listed below are different kinds of regions in the United States. Identify the kind of region by filling in the proper circle. Some regions may be identified by more than one feature.

	Government	Where People Live	Physical Features	Economy	Culture
a. Coastal Plain	○	○	●	○	○
b. an Amish community	○	●	○	○	●
c. county	●	○	○	○	○
d. manufacturing region	○	○	○	●	○
e. suburb	○	●	○	○	○
f. desert	○	○	●	○	○
g. school district	●	●	○	○	○
h. a Mexican American neighborhood	○	●	○	○	●
i. mining region	○	○	○	●	○
j. tourism region	○	○	○	●	○
k. Piedmont	○	○	●	○	○

23 **ESSAY** (10 points)

Interdependence among different regions of the United States is possible partly because of the country's modern transportation system. In a one-paragraph essay, explain two ways that transportation helps connect people in the United States.

Students' responses should show an understanding of how transportation allows people in different regions in the United States to trade goods and services faster, more easily, and less expensively. Students should also mention that modern transportation allows people to visit family and friends in different regions of the country and the world. Some forms of transportation students may include are cars, trucks, boats, trains, and airplanes.

8 ■ Assessment Program   Chapter 2 Test

ANSWERS

1 Test

Part One: Test Your Understanding

MULTIPLE CHOICE (2 points each)

Directions Circle the letter of the best answer.

1. The global address of the United States includes which of the following hemispheres?
   - **(A)** Northern and Western Hemispheres
   - B Southern and Western Hemispheres
   - C Northern and Eastern Hemispheres
   - D Northern and Southern Hemispheres

2. What country forms much of the northern border of the United States?
   - F Mexico
   - G England
   - H Spain
   - **(J)** Canada

3. Which of the following is *not* an example of a landform?
   - A valley
   - **(B)** tributary
   - C plain
   - D mountain

4. Which of these mountain ranges is *not* located in the western United States?
   - **(F)** Appalachian Mountains
   - G Coast Ranges
   - H Sierra Nevada
   - J Cascade Range

5. The place where a river begins is called—
   - A its channel.
   - B its mouth.
   - C its drainage basin.
   - **(D)** its source.

6. Which of these statements best describes how a river erodes the land?
   - F The river leaves silt at its mouth, forming a delta.
   - G When the river's current slows down, it forms sandbars.
   - H The river leaves silt on floodplains after a flood.
   - **(J)** The movement of water wears away Earth's surface.

7. The weather of a place over a long time is its—
   - **(A)** climate.
   - B humidity.
   - C precipitation.
   - D habitat.

8. How can an ocean affect climate?
   - **(F)** It can make a place cooler in summer and warmer in winter.
   - G It can make the air drier.
   - H It can make the winter longer.
   - J It can affect the amount of sunlight reaching a place.

9. Which of these is a way to conserve resources?
   - A removing insulation
   - **(B)** recycling products
   - C driving more often
   - D drinking bottled water

10. Which of these regions has an exact boundary and its own government?
    - F a city
    - G a county
    - H a state
    - **(J)** all of them

11. Which of the following is a manufacturing job?
    - **(A)** sewing clothes
    - B cleaning houses
    - C cutting hair
    - D delivering mail

12. Which of the following is *not* a service job?
    - F repairing cars
    - G caring for sick people
    - **(H)** farming
    - J delivering mail

13. Why do people in different regions depend on one another?
    - **(A)** Each region needs resources and products from other regions.
    - B All regions have the same needs.
    - C Some regions have more money than other regions.
    - D Resources and goods are divided evenly among regions.

(continued)

Unit 1 Test — Assessment Program ■ 9
10 ■ Assessment Program — Unit 1 Test

COMPLETION (2 points each)

Directions Fill in the blank with the correct term from the list below. You will not use two terms.

channel	fuel	industry
mineral	mouth	peninsula
rural	technology	urban

14. Land that is almost completely surrounded by water is a __peninsula__.

15. The deepest part of a river or other body of water is called its __channel__.

16. People use metals from __mineral__ resources to make wire, pots, pans, coins, and other products.

17. Most people in the United States live in __urban__ regions.

18. Many people in __rural__ regions earn their livings as farmers.

19. An __industry__ is all the businesses that make one kind of product or provide one kind of service.

20. Computers, fax machines, and telephones are examples of __technology__.

(continued)

Unit 1 Test — Assessment Program ■ 11

SHORT ANSWER (2 points each)

Directions Write the answer to each question on the lines provided.

21. What are the highest and lowest points in North America, and where are they located?

   Mt. McKinley, in Alaska, is the highest point in North America. Death Valley, in California, is the lowest point in North America.

22. Why is fertile soil an important natural resource?

   Possible response: People use soil to grow the food we eat and to grow trees for lumber and wood products.

23. Why do most people live in more than one region at the same time?

   Possible response: Most regions do not have exact boundaries, so they often overlap. Regions where people live often belong to a neighborhood, city, county, and state all at the same time.

24. What are some major industries in the United States?

   Possible responses: agriculture, mining, lumber, fishing, manufacturing, service industries

25. What are some forms of transportation in the United States?

   Possible responses: cars, trucks, buses, trains, subways, boats, airplanes

(continued)

12 ■ Assessment Program — Unit 1 Test

© Harcourt

ANSWERS

Part Two: Test Your Skills

READ AN ELEVATION MAP (2 points each)

Directions Use the map below to answer the questions that follow.

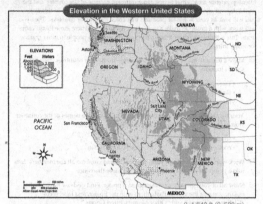

Elevation in the Western United States

0–1,640 ft (0–500 m)

26 What is the elevation of the land along most of the Pacific Coast?

27 Where in the western United States is the elevation of the land below sea level?

in southern California near the United States-Mexico border (in Death Valley)

28 What river's source is at a higher elevation, the Sacramento River's or the

Colorado River's? the Colorado River's source

29 Why do you think the elevation of the land in most of western Colorado,

Wyoming, and New Mexico is above 6,500 feet (2,000 m)? because the Rocky

Mountains run through that part of the western United States

(continued)

Part Three: Apply What You Have Learned

Directions Complete each of the following activities.

30 **SEQUENCE IMPORTANT EVENTS IN UNITED STATES HISTORY** (4 points)

On the lines next to the events below, write the numbers 1 through 4 to indicate the order in which those events occurred.

a. __3__ The name America appeared on a map for the first time.

b. __2__ Christopher Columbus sailed to North America from Spain.

c. __4__ People came from all over the world to live in the United States.

d. __1__ The ancestors of Native Americans may have walked across an isthmus from Asia to North America.

31 **SEQUENCE A RIVER'S PATH** (4 points)

Order the steps below to show how water flows across the land in rivers. On the lines next to the steps, write the numbers 1 through 4 to show the correct order of the steps.

a. __1__ Drops of rain start to fall on the ground.

b. __3__ Water in the river carves a path, or channel, through the land.

c. __2__ The water runs down Earth's surface and becomes part of a river.

d. __4__ The water reaches the river's mouth and empties into a larger body of water.

32 **SEQUENCE REGIONS BY SIZE** (6 points)

Identify the usual size of regions from largest (1) to smallest (6) by writing the numbers 1 through 6 on the lines next to the regions below.

a. __1__ country   b. __5__ neighborhood

c. __3__ county   d. __4__ city

e. __2__ state   f. __6__ street

(continued)

---

33 **MAP REGIONS AROUND THE WORLD** (11 points)

Directions On the map below, each of Earth's oceans is labeled with a letter. Write the name of each ocean on the line beside its matching letter.

OCEANS

A. Pacific Ocean   B. Atlantic Ocean

C. Indian Ocean   D. Arctic Ocean

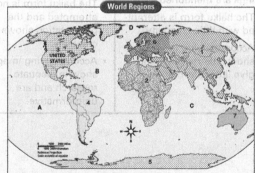

World Regions

Directions Listed below are Earth's continents. Locate each continent on the map above and label it with the correct number.
Labels are shown on the map.

CONTINENTS

1. Asia   2. Africa   3. North America
4. South America   5. Antarctica   6. Europe
7. Australia

---

34 **CATEGORIZE NATURAL RESOURCES AND THE ECONOMY** (7 points)

Complete the table below by listing the kinds of jobs people in the United States might have that use each natural resource.

Natural Resource	Jobs
Salt water	Possible response: fisher
Soil	Possible response: farmer
Forests	Possible response: carpenter
Minerals	Possible response: miner
Fuels	Possible response: oil driller
Fresh water	Possible response: power plant operator
Grasslands	Possible response: dairy farmer

35 **ESSAY** (10 points)

In a one-paragraph essay, name and describe four different regions in which you live.

Responses will vary. The regions where the students live may be based on climate, natural resources, natural vegetation, government, way of life, language, religion, or other features.

© Harcourt

ANSWERS

Name _____ Date _____

Individual Performance Task
Landform Poems

In this task, you will use what you learned in Unit 1 to write and illustrate a haiku about the geography of the United States. A haiku is a short Japanese poem using words that do not rhyme. It often describes nature or someone's feelings about nature. A haiku has just three lines. The first line has five syllables, or parts of words. The second line has seven syllables, and the last line has five. Haikus usually do not capitalize the first letter of each line or use a period, comma, or other punctuation at the end of each line. For example:

the United States	← 5 syllables
has many landforms, climates,	← 7 syllables
regions, and people	← 5 syllables

1 Choose a landform that you read about in Unit 1 to be the subject of your haiku.

2 Write a first draft of your haiku. It should tell something about the landform—where it is located, its features, or why you chose it for your poem. You can use your textbook or library resources to write the haiku.

3 Review your haiku to be sure that it has the correct number of lines and the correct number of syllables in each line.

4 Illustrate your haiku with pictures from magazines or newspapers, or draw your own pictures.

5 Read your haiku to the class, and explain how your illustrations relate to the poem.

Unit 1 Test   Assessment Program ▪ 17

Name _____ Date _____

Group Performance Task
World Products

Interdependence means that people from different regions of the country and the world depend on one another for resources, products, and services. In this task, you will look in your home for products that come from other countries. Then you will work with a group to make a map and a list to show where these things came from. This activity will show that each person depends on people in other regions for many things.

1 Make a list of items in your home that come from other countries. Your list should include

  • three pieces of clothing
  • three food products
  • three other kinds of manufactured goods

Your list should have the names of the products and the names of the countries from which they came. One list might include

  • sneakers—Korea   • T-shirt—Mexico
  • cookies—Canada   • television—Japan

2 Work with a small group of your classmates, and combine all the members' lists into a group list. Do not list the same item more than once.

3 Show all of your group's information on a poster. Find or draw three blank outline maps of the world. Paste them onto the poster, and label them "Clothing," "Foods," and "Other Manufactured Goods."

4 Use a color to shade in the countries from which your group's products came. Use a different color for each map. Make a map key for each map. In each map key, draw a symbol that represents each product. Place each map key symbol on the country where that product was made.

5 Present your poster to the class. Discuss with your classmates the kinds of things—from other countries—that all of you use. Listen as the other groups present their lists and maps. As a class, organize all the items in the lists by the continents from which they came. Discuss why certain items are likely to come from certain places around the world.

18 ▪ Assessment Program   Unit 1 Test

INDIVIDUAL PERFORMANCE TASK

Score 4	Score 3	Score 2	Score 1
• The landform and key details or feelings are clearly identified. • The haiku form is followed and the poem shows excellent creativity. • Supporting images reflect excellent research and are very informative.	• The landform and some details or feelings are identified. • The haiku form is followed and shows some creativity. • Supporting images show good research and are informative.	• The landform and some general features or feelings are mentioned. • The haiku form is attempted with little creativity. • Accompanying images show little research and give little information.	• No specific details or feelings are presented. • The haiku form is not attempted and the presentation shows no creativity. • Accompanying images show inadequate research and are uninformative.

GROUP PERFORMANCE TASK

Score 4	Score 3	Score 2	Score 1
• Poster shows a full list of items carefully related to the world maps. • Information on the poster is clearly presented. • Details on the poster reflect careful research and thought.	• Poster shows a good list of items well related to the world maps. • Information on the poster is generally clear. • Details on the poster reflect some research and thought.	• Poster shows a small list of items vaguely related to the world maps. • Information on the poster is not very clear. • Details on the poster reflect little research or thought.	• Poster shows a few items poorly related to the world maps. • Information on the poster is unclear and inaccurate. • Details on the poster reflect no research or consideration.

ANSWER KEY

ANSWERS

Name _____ Date _____

3 Test

Part One: Test Your Understanding

MULTIPLE CHOICE (4 points each)

Directions Circle the letter of the best answer.

1. The explorer who named New England was—
   A Christopher Columbus.
   (B) John Smith.
   C Samuel de Champlain.
   D Amerigo Vespucci.

2. Which of the following is *not* a New England state?
   F New Hampshire
   G Connecticut
   H Rhode Island
   (J) New Jersey

3. Which of these natural resources did Native Americans in New England use to survive?
   A silver and gold
   B cattle and sheep
   C granite and marble
   (D) fish and berries

4. Why did the Pilgrims leave England and sail to North America?
   F They were searching for gold.
   (G) They wanted to practice their religion freely.
   H They wanted to meet new people.
   J They were searching for new trade opportunities.

5. Where were most of New England's earliest settlements built?
   (A) along bays of the Atlantic Coast
   B in the Connecticut River valley
   C along the shores of Lake Champlain
   D in the Green and White Mountains

6. Which of the following was *not* a major industry in colonial New England?
   F agriculture
   G shipping
   H fishing
   (J) mining

(continued)

Chapter 3 Test   Assessment Program ▪ 19

Name _____ Date _____

7. Why were most early factories built along rivers?
   (A) to use the power of the rushing water to run machines
   B to be closer to the resources they used
   C to be closer to their customers
   D to provide drinking water for factory workers

8. Which of these makes up the largest part of New England's economy today?
   F textile industries
   (G) service industries
   H shipping industries
   J agricultural industries

9. What do citizens accomplish during town meetings?
   A They determine the population of their town.
   (B) They make important decisions about their town.
   C They learn about other New England towns.
   D They organize volunteers for town services.

IDENTIFICATION (4 points each)

Directions For each group of terms, circle the letter of the term that does *not* belong with the other two.

10. a. granite   (b.) colony   c. quarry
11. a. cape   b. harbor   (c.) common
12. a. industrial economy   (b.) sap   c. textile mill
13. (a.) recreation   b. specialize   c. fish farm
14. a. cranberries   b. potatoes   (c.) cotton

(continued)

20 ▪ Assessment Program   Chapter 3 Test

Name _____ Date _____

Part Two: Test Your Skills

READ A TIME LINE (3 points each)

Directions Use the time line at the bottom of this page to answer the following questions.

15. What centuries are shown on this time line? the eighteenth, nineteenth, and twentieth centuries

16. Into what equal time periods is this time line divided (from one white line to the next)? 50 years

17. Why is 1774 an important year in Newfane's history? That was the year Newfane was founded and the year that Newfane's first town meeting was held.

18. How many years was the railroad in operation in Newfane? 56 years

19. After what year would a visitor see electric lights in Newfane? 1913

20. Which was built first, Newfane's Union Hall or Newfane's Moore Free Library? the Union Hall

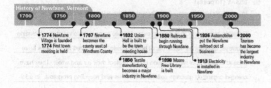

(continued)

Chapter 3 Test   Assessment Program ▪ 21

Name _____ Date _____

Part Three: Apply What You Have Learned

Directions Complete each of the following activities.

21. **CATEGORIZE PRODUCTS** (8 points)

List the products that people in New England produce using each of the following natural resources. Possible responses are given below.

NATURAL RESOURCE	PRODUCTS
Trees	lumber, paper products, maple syrup, fruit
Soil	crops such as potatoes, cranberries, corn, and mushrooms; raising sheep, hogs, and dairy cows on thick grasses

22. **COMPARE AND CONTRAST TOWNS AND VILLAGES AROUND THE WORLD** (8 points)

List four things that these towns and villages have in common: Newfane, Vermont; Hawkshead, England; Tenterfield, Australia; St. Andrews, Canada.

Possible responses: They are all small towns or villages. People in each place speak English. They were all settled by the British. They all have town commons or squares. Tourism is a major industry in all of those places. They all have old buildings. Some students may make specific comparisons between two places. For instance, people in Newfane and in Tenterfield make decisions at town meetings; or Newfane and Hawkshead both lie on rolling hills covered with grassy fields and trees.

23. **ESSAY** (10 points)

In a one-paragraph essay, describe the major differences between coastal New England and the New England countryside.

Possible response: The land in coastal New England is rocky in the north and a coastal plain in the south. The New England countryside is a land of green valleys, rolling hills, and low mountain ranges. Most people in coastal New England live in busy urban areas, while many people in the New England countryside live in quiet small towns. Most people in coastal New England work in service industries. However, many people in the New England countryside still use the land to earn a living.

22 ▪ Assessment Program   Chapter 3 Test

© Harcourt

ANSWERS

Name _____ Date _____

4 Test

Part One: Test Your Understanding

MULTIPLE CHOICE (4 points each)

Directions Circle the letter of the best answer.

1 Henry Hudson was—
 A the leader of the Quakers.
 B one of the first Europeans to start a colony in North America.
 C one of the first Europeans to explore the Middle Atlantic region.
 D the person who named New York and New Jersey.

2 A loosely united group of governments working together is called a—
 F Society of Friends.
 G colony.
 H confederation.
 J treaty.

3 Which of the following is *not* a way that the Middle Atlantic Colonies were like the United States today?
 A The colonies welcomed people of all religions.
 B Farming was the largest part of the colonies' economy.
 C The largest cities were located along major waterways.
 D The colonies had a mix of people from different countries.

4 Which of the following is *not* a reason why the colonists decided to declare their independence from Britain?
 F The colonists had no representation in the British government.
 G New British laws made it difficult for the colonists to trade.
 H The British protected the colonists' trade and coasts.
 J New British laws forced the colonists to pay heavy taxes.

5 The Declaration of Independence states that—
 A Washington, D.C., would become the nation's capital.
 B all people have the right to life, liberty, and the pursuit of happiness.
 C all people should receive equal amounts of money.
 D Britain would give the colonists representation in their government.

(continued)

Chapter 4 Test

Name _____ Date _____

6 Which of these port cities grew up on a harbor at the mouth of the Hudson River?
 F Philadelphia
 G Pittsburgh
 H Buffalo
 J New York City

7 The Erie Canal connected the Great Lakes to what body of water?
 A the Mississippi River
 B the Atlantic Ocean
 C the St. Lawrence River
 D the Pacific Ocean

8 Which of these resources is *not* needed to produce steel?
 F iron
 G oil
 H limestone
 J coal

9 Why did many immigrants move to Middle Atlantic cities during the late 1800s and early 1900s?
 A for low-cost housing
 B for factory jobs
 C to buy farmland
 D for service industry jobs

MATCHING (4 points each)

Directions Match each term on the right with its meaning. Then write the correct letter in the space provided.

		Meaning		Term
10	E	a trading center where ships are loaded and unloaded		A. commute
11	D	deep and wide enough for ships to use		B. competition
12	B	the contest among companies to get the most customers or sell the most products		C. metropolitan area
13	C	a large city together with its suburbs		D. navigable
14	A	to travel back and forth each day		E. port

(continued)

Chapter 4 Test

Name _____ Date _____

Part Two: Test Your Skills

IDENTIFY FACT AND OPINION (2 points each)

Directions Read the following statements about the Middle Atlantic region and decide whether they are facts or opinions. In the space next to each entry, write *F* if it is a statement of fact. Write *O* if it is a statement of opinion.

15 _F_ New Amsterdam was the capital of the Dutch colony in the Middle Atlantic region.

16 _O_ Religious freedom was the most important reason people settled in the Middle Atlantic Colonies.

17 _F_ The Middle Atlantic Colonies were called the "breadbasket" colonies because they produced so much wheat.

18 _O_ The Middle Atlantic Colonies were better than the New England Colonies.

19 _F_ The Erie Canal helped trade grow in the Middle Atlantic region.

20 _F_ The United States officially became an independent nation in 1783.

21 _O_ An interstate highway is the most beautiful route for road travel.

22 _F_ Steel was used to build railroad tracks, bridges, buildings, ships, and tools.

23 _O_ New York City is the most exciting city in the United States.

24 _F_ More people in the Middle Atlantic states live in cities than in rural areas.

(continued)

Chapter 4 Test

Name _____ Date _____

Part Three: Apply What You Have Learned

Directions Complete each of the following activities.

25 SUMMARIZE TRANSPORTATION AND GROWTH (8 points)

In the space below, list four major forms of transportation that have helped the Middle Atlantic states grow and connect.

Possible responses include canals, seaways, railroads with high-speed trains, highways, airplanes, and subways.

26 SUMMARIZE THE PROBLEMS AND BENEFITS OF CITIES (6 points)

Though cities have much to offer, there are problems for people who live in them. List three benefits and three problems for people living in cities.
Possible responses are given.

BENEFITS OF CITY LIVING	PROBLEMS OF CITY LIVING
job and educational opportunities; different kinds of food, dance, and music; professional sports teams; entertainment; services; public transportation	crowding; traffic; pollution; unemployment; providing services for such large populations; small or expensive housing

27 ESSAY (10 points)

In a one-paragraph essay, describe some of the actions that cities around the world have taken to solve urban problems.

Possible response: Cities have provided public transportation systems including subways, high-speed trains, canal boats, buses, and shared taxis. Cities have passed laws to deal with pollution and to protect their air and water. They have created organized garbage collection services and recycling programs. In addition, some cities have come up with special solutions to urban problems. These include Amsterdam's White Bikes program, Mexico City's license plate programs, and Tokyo's sleeping capsules and bullet trains.

© Harcourt

Chapter 4 Test

ANSWERS

Name _____ Date _____

2 Test

Part One: Test Your Understanding

MULTIPLE CHOICE (2 points each)

Directions Circle the letter of the best answer.

1. Why did the Pilgrims and Puritans settle in North America?
   A because of the continent's many natural resources
   B to start shipbuilding and fishing industries
   C to trade with Native Americans for furs
   (D) to practice their religions freely

2. A colony is—
   (F) a settlement started by people who leave their country to live in another place.
   G a point of land reaching out into the ocean.
   H a person who comes to live in a country from some other place.
   J a loosely united group of governments working together.

3. In an industrial economy—
   A most people work along major rivers.
   B people do not need farms and farmers.
   C factories do not need raw materials.
   (D) most goods are made in factories.

4. The first factory in the United States was built by Samuel Slater to produce—
   (F) textiles.
   G lumber.
   H steel.
   J flour.

5. The poor, rocky soil of New England is a result of—
   A winds blowing the soil away.
   B rivers eroding away the soil.
   (C) glaciers moving across the land.
   D inefficient farming methods.

6. Which of the following is *not* a way that the Middle Atlantic Colonies differed from the New England Colonies?
   F People from many different countries came to live in the Middle Atlantic Colonies.
   G The Middle Atlantic Colonies welcomed people of all religions.
   H Much of the Middle Atlantic region has fertile soil.
   (J) The Middle Atlantic Colonies had many busy ports.

(continued)

Name _____ Date _____

7. Why do some historians call Philadelphia the birthplace of the United States?
   A The first colony was started there.
   (B) The Declaration of Independence was signed there.
   C The first fighting of the American Revolution took place there.
   D It was the largest trading center in the American colonies.

8. When the United States first became a nation, what formed its western boundary?
   (F) the Mississippi River
   G the Atlantic Ocean
   H the Appalachian Mountains
   J the Great Lakes

9. Why did western Pennsylvania become a leading steel-producing region?
   A It had a large population to supply workers for steel mills.
   (B) It was surrounded by all of the natural resources needed to produce steel.
   C It was linked to the Atlantic Ocean by the St. Lawrence Seaway.
   D People used steel to build railroads, machines, and tall buildings.

10. Why are New York City, Philadelphia, and Boston important centers of trade?
    F Many people work in these cities.
    (G) They are all built on major waterways.
    H They are all surrounded by large farming areas.
    J They are all located along the Erie Canal.

11. Traffic, pollution, and trash in cities are all problems that are made worse by—
    A climate.
    (B) crowding.
    C unemployment.
    D tenements.

(continued)

Name _____ Date _____

MATCHING (2 points each)

Directions Match each term on the right with its meaning. Then write the correct letter in the space provided.

	Meaning		Term
12.	D	a place where ships can dock safely	A. quarry
13.	A	a large, open pit cut into the ground from which stone is mined	B. urban sprawl
14.	E	to work at only one kind of job and do it well	C. turnpike
15.	F	in a river, a rocky place where a sudden drop in elevation causes fast-moving, dangerous water	D. harbor
16.	C	a road that drivers must pay to use	E. specialize
17.	B	the spreading of urban areas and the growth of new centers of business and shopping	F. rapids

SHORT ANSWER (4 points each)

Directions Write the answer to each question on the lines provided.

18. How did the Appalachian Mountains affect early water travel in the Northeast?
    They separated rivers that flowed into the Great Lakes from those that flowed into the Atlantic Ocean. There was no navigable route across the region.

19. Why do steel mills in the Northeast no longer produce as much steel as they once did?
    Steel mills in other regions can produce steel more cheaply, and steel industries in the Northeast face strong competition from steelmakers in other countries.

20. What kinds of jobs do many people have in cities in the Northeast?
    jobs in ports, factories, governments, and other service industries

(continued)

Name _____ Date _____

Part Two: Test Your Skills

USE A ROAD MAP AND MILEAGE TABLE

Directions Use the map and mileage table on page 31 to answer the following questions. (3 points each)

21. Which interstate highway connects Philadelphia, New York City, and Boston?
    Interstate 95

22. How many miles separate Philadelphia and Pittsburgh, Pennsylvania? What highway could you take to travel from Philadelphia to Pittsburgh?
    288 miles; Interstate 76

23. How many miles is it from New York City to Dover?
    160 miles

24. Which cities are farther apart, Boston and New York City or Pittsburgh and New York City?
    Pittsburgh and New York City

25. Which interstate highway follows the southern shore of Lake Erie?
    Interstate 90

(continued)

© Harcourt

ANSWERS

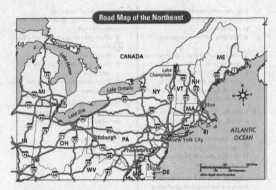

Road Map of the Northeast

NORTHEAST ROAD MILEAGE					
	Boston, MA	Dover, DE	New York City, NY	Philadelphia, PA	Pittsburgh, PA
Boston, MA		378	206	296	561
Dover, DE	378		160	74	332
New York City, NY	206	160		91	368
Philadelphia, PA	296	74	91		288
Pittsburgh, PA	561	332	368	288	

(continued)

Part Three: Apply What You Have Learned

Directions Complete each of the following activities.

㉖ **IDENTIFY CAUSES AND EFFECTS** (8 points)

Complete the chart below to describe some of the causes and effects of changes and events that have occurred in the Northeast.
Possible responses are given.

CAUSE	→	EFFECT
Huge glaciers moved across New England thousands of years ago.	→	Much of New England was left with poor, rocky soil.
The Middle Atlantic Colonies welcomed people from many countries and people of many religions.	→	The Middle Atlantic Colonies had a mix of people and cultures.
Many cities in the Northeast were built at the mouths of large rivers.	→	Many cities in the Northeast are busy ports.
The colonists won the American Revolution against Britain and signed a treaty ending the war.	→	The United States became an independent nation.
People built the Erie Canal.	→	Trade increased in the Northeast, and New York City became the country's leading trading city.
Millions of immigrants moved to cities in the Northeast.	→	Cities in the Northeast grew rapidly, have a mix of cultures, and are crowded.
Western Pennsylvania is surrounded by coal, iron, and limestone; it has transportation links.	→	Western Pennsylvania became the center of the nation's steel industry.
Cities in the Northeast spread out and grew over time.	→	The largest megalopolis in the nation is located in the Northeast.

(continued)

㉗ **IDENTIFY LOCATIONS ON A MAP** (9 points)

Write the letters of the places listed below next to the numbers on the map to show the location of each place.

A. Albany, NY   B. Erie Canal   C. New York City
D. Appalachian Mountains   E. Hudson River   F. St. Lawrence Seaway
G. Buffalo, NY   H. Lake Erie   I. Atlantic Ocean

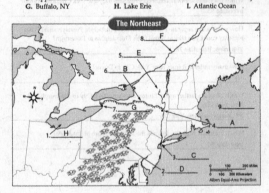

The Northeast

(continued)

㉘ **MAKE GENERALIZATIONS ABOUT LIFE IN NEW ENGLAND** (12 points)

List four ways people in New England have adapted to the region's cool climate and rocky soil in order to make a living. Possible responses are given.

People grow crops that do well in those conditions, such as cranberries, blueberries, potatoes, apples, and greenhouse crops.

People raise dairy cows and sheep on the thick pasture grasses.

People mine granite, marble, and other kinds of stone in quarries.

People use forests for lumber industries and to manufacture wood products and maple syrup.

People use the oceans, bays, and rivers to earn a living.

㉙ **ESSAY** (10 points)

In a one-paragraph essay, describe some of the similarities and differences between the New England states and the Middle Atlantic states.

Possible response: Both the New England states and the Middle Atlantic states lie in the northeastern United States along the Atlantic Coast. Both have many ports and other large cities. Millions of immigrants have moved to both regions over time. Service industries make up the largest part of the economy in both regions. The soil in most of the Middle Atlantic region is more fertile than the soil in most of New England. The Middle Atlantic region lies farther south, so it generally has a warmer climate than New England does. Most of the early settlers in New England came from England, while people from many different countries settled in the Middle Atlantic Colonies.

© Harcourt

ANSWERS

Individual Performance Task

And Now a Word About the Erie Canal

Your task is to write a newspaper advertisement for the newly opened Erie Canal. In your advertisement you are trying to get businesses to use the canal to ship their products. You can use facts from the box below to make your advertisement.

FACTS ABOUT THE ERIE CANAL

Length—363 miles
Width—42 miles
Depth—4 feet
Number of locks—83
Western end—Buffalo, New York
Middle—Syracuse, New York
Eastern end—Troy, New York
Nickname—"The Big Ditch"
Average speed for boats traveling on the Erie Canal—5 miles per hour
Time from Albany to Buffalo by horse—20 days
Time from Albany to Buffalo by canal—6 days

❶ Gather information about the Erie Canal from your textbook and from other sources.

❷ Write a first draft of your newspaper advertisement. Be creative, but make sure you are historically accurate.

❸ Review your advertisement to be sure you have included all the important information. Draw a picture to illustrate your advertisement.

❹ Have a classmate read your advertisement to see whether any part is unclear. If necessary, revise your advertisement.

❺ Share the advertisement with your class, and then display it so that other students can read it.

Group Performance Task

Town Meeting

The first recorded town meeting in New England was held in Dorchester, Massachusetts, in 1633. Since then, people in many New England towns have held town meetings to make important decisions. In this task, you will hold a mock town meeting to make decisions about your class.

❶ With your small group, identify an issue or a problem you would like to present in the meeting. For example, you may wish to change the arrangement of the desks in the classroom. Or you may want to organize a canned-food drive for needy families, a homework support group, or a class party.

❷ Gather information about your group's issue or problem, and write a short description of how you would like to address or solve it. For the issue of the desk arrangement, for instance, you may want to make a diagram of the present arrangement and another to show the way your group wants the desks to be rearranged. You may take a survey of your classmates to get their opinions about the issue. You could also speak to your teacher and principal.

❸ As a class, hold your town meeting. Ask your teacher to conduct the meeting. One student from each group should be that group's representative, and the other students should take notes to record what happens in the meeting. Representatives should take turns presenting their issues to the class. Then the class should vote on the issue each representative presents.

❹ Return to your group, and write a brief summary of what was decided in the meeting concerning your issue.

❺ As a class, compile the group summaries into a class meeting announcement. Post your announcement outside your classroom. That way, students who did not attend the meeting can learn about the decisions that were made.

INDIVIDUAL PERFORMANCE TASK

Score 4	Score 3	Score 2	Score 1
• Key facts are incorporated accurately in the advertisement. • Images and other information are very well researched. • Presentation is creative and highly appealing.	• Useful facts are included in the advertisement. • Images and other information reflect good research. • Presentation shows some creativity and is fairly appealing.	• Few facts are included in the advertisement. • Images and other information reflect little research. • Presentation is weak and lacking in appeal.	• Facts are limited and uninformative. • Other elements are inaccurate and show no real research. • Presentation is unimaginative.

GROUP PERFORMANCE TASK

Score 4	Score 3	Score 2	Score 1
• Individual discussions show a deep understanding of the issues. • Participation is cooperative and helpful. • Information given shows thorough preparation and research. • Final summaries reflect thoughtful contribution.	• Individual discussions show general understanding of the issues. • Participation is intermittent. • Information given shows some preparation and research. • Final summaries reflect a modest contribution.	• Individual discussions show little understanding of the issues. • Participation is only occasional. • Information given shows little preparation or research. • Final summaries reflect little contribution.	• Individual discussions show almost no understanding of the issues. • Participation is very limited. • Information given shows no preparation or research. • Final summaries reflect no contribution.

ANSWERS

Name _____ Date _____

5 Test

Part One: Test Your Understanding
MULTIPLE CHOICE (4 points each)

Directions Circle the letter of the best answer.

1 Where did Europeans first settle in the Atlantic Coast and Appalachian region?
A along the Mississippi River
(B) along the Coastal Plain
C on the Piedmont
D on the Cumberland Plateau

2 Why is Roanoke often called the "Lost Colony"?
F All of the first colonists of Roanoke died from starvation.
(G) No one knows why the first colonists of Roanoke disappeared.
H Roanoke Island is difficult to find on a map.
J The first Roanoke colonists lost all of their belongings in a hurricane.

3 To run machines, early settlers along the Fall Line used—
(A) waterpower.
B coal.
C natural gas.
D oil.

4 How did most early settlers cross the Appalachian Mountains to reach present-day Kentucky and Tennessee?
F by riding boats upriver from the Coastal Plain
(G) by walking or riding wagons through the Cumberland Gap
H by riding trains over the mountains
J by traveling up the Mississippi River from the Gulf of Mexico

5 In the past, why did many people in Appalachia make most of the things they needed?
A because craft products were popular items at festivals
B because they had few natural resources available
(C) because travel and trade were difficult in the mountains
D because they could not sell the products they made

(continued)

Chapter 5 Test   Assessment Program ▪ 37

Name _____ Date _____

6 How did the Tennessee Valley Authority, or TVA, help the Atlantic Coast and Appalachian region grow?
(F) It built dams and power plants to supply water and electricity.
G It organized groups of settlers to move to the region.
H It cleared more land for farmers to plant crops in the region.
J It opened coal mines in the region, creating more jobs.

7 In which of the following states is coal mining a major industry?
A Maryland and Virginia
B Tennessee and North Carolina
(C) West Virginia and Kentucky
D Virginia and North Carolina

8 Which of the following is *not* a way in which government has helped some cities in the Atlantic Coast and Appalachian states grow?
F State capitals were located in some cities in the region.
G The national government is based in Washington, D.C.
(H) Government-owned high-tech industries are growing rapidly in the region.
J The government built some of the nation's largest military bases in the region.

MATCHING (4 points each)

Directions Match each term on the right with its meaning. Then write the correct letter in the space provided.

Meaning	Term
9 C a place where rivers drop from higher to lower land	A. pass
10 D a person who first settles a new place	B. resort
11 A an opening between high mountains	C. fall line
12 F a lake that stores water held back by a dam	D. pioneer
13 H a metal used to make things that need to be strong and light	E. reclaim
14 E to return something, such as land, to its natural condition	F. reservoir
15 B a place where people go to relax and have fun	G. wildlife refuge
16 G an area of land set aside to protect animals and other living things	H. aluminum

(continued)

38 ▪ Assessment Program   Chapter 5 Test

Name _____ Date _____

Part Two: Test Your Skills
READ A LINE GRAPH (4 points each)

Directions Use the line graph to answer these questions.

17 About how many people lived in Virginia in 1850?
about 1 million people

18 In which year was the population of Virginia the highest? the lowest?
2000; 1800

19 In which 50-year period did the greatest change in population take place?
1950 to 2000

20 What general statement can you make about Virginia's population, based on the line graph?
Possible response: The population of Virginia has constantly increased since 1800.

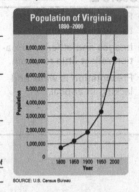

Population of Virginia
1800–2000

SOURCE: U.S. Census Bureau

21 Based on the line graph, what prediction can you make about the population of Virginia in 2050?
Possible responses: The population of Virginia in 2050 will be greater than in 2000; the population of Virginia in 2050 will be greater than 7 million; the population will continue to increase through the year 2050.

Chapter 5 Test   Assessment Program ▪ 39

Name _____ Date _____

Part Three: Apply What You Have Learned

Directions Complete each of the following activities.

22 COMPARE AND CONTRAST INFORMATION (6 points)
Maryland, Virginia, and North Carolina are called the Atlantic Coast states, and West Virginia, Kentucky, and Tennessee are called the Appalachian states. Use the Venn diagram below to list four ways in which those state groups are the same and two ways in which they are different. Possible responses are given.

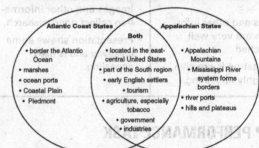

23 ESSAY (10 points)
In a one-paragraph essay, explain why many cities in the Atlantic Coast and Appalachian states have grown up along rivers.
Possible response: During colonial days, people settled near rivers to have drinking water and a means of transportation. Later, they settled farther inland along rivers to use waterpower to run machines and ship products to markets. Today cities along rivers continue to grow as centers of shipping and trade.
Because many rivers in the region have been dammed, new industries have also started near rivers to use the hydroelectric power. As a result, many people have moved to those cities along rivers for factory jobs.

40 ▪ Assessment Program   Chapter 5 Test

© Harcourt

ANSWERS

Name _____ Date _____

6 Test

Part One: Test Your Understanding

MULTIPLE CHOICE (4 points each)

Directions Circle the letter of the best answer.

1 Which state did Spanish explorer Ponce de León name in 1513?
A South Carolina
B Georgia
C Florida
D Alabama

2 How did early farmers use rivers in the Southeast and Gulf region?
F to irrigate their crops in the dry climate
G to ship their crops to markets
H to run mills to grind their wheat into flour
J to create hydroelectric power

3 Which of the following is *not* a way in which the North and South differed before the Civil War?
A More people in the North were moving to cities.
B More people in the North owned slaves.
C More people in the North wanted to abolish slavery.
D More people in the North worked in factories.

4 What effect did the Emancipation Proclamation eventually have?
F The American Civil War ended.
G Eleven Southern states seceded from the Union.
H All slaves in areas fighting the Union were given their freedom.
J Cotton plantations were made illegal in the South.

5 Which of these processed foods does *not* use a major crop grown in the Southeast and Gulf states?
A sugar
B peanut butter
C orange juice
D popcorn

6 Which of these cities in the Southeast and Gulf states is *not* a port city?
F Charleston, South Carolina
G Atlanta, Georgia
H Mobile, Alabama
J Miami, Florida

7 Which of the following best describes the location of the Sun Belt?
A in the southern part of the United States
B in the northern part of the United States
C along the Atlantic Coast of the United States
D along the Pacific Coast of the United States

8 Which of these islands or island groups is made of coral?
F Hilton Head Island
G Puerto Rico
H the Florida Keys
J the U.S. Virgin Islands

9 What do Brazil, India, and Greece all have in common with the Southeast and Gulf states?
A tropical storms
B coastal regions
C fertile land
D barrier islands

TRUE OR FALSE (3 points each)

Directions Read each of the statements below about the Southeast and Gulf states. In the space next to each, write *T* if the statement is true. Write *F* if the statement is false.

10 __T__ People from Spain were the first Europeans to explore the region.

11 __F__ The region has a short growing season and plentiful rainfall.

12 __T__ Some early farmers in the region started plantations.

13 __T__ All of the Southeast and Gulf states were part of the Confederacy.

14 __F__ The region has few harbors or navigable rivers.

15 __T__ Retired people make up a large part of the region's population.

16 __T__ Hundreds of islands lie along the region's coasts.

17 __F__ People use the region's forests to produce textiles.

(continued)

Name _____ Date _____

Part Two: Test Your Skills

COMPARE MAPS WITH DIFFERENT SCALES (4 points each)

Directions Study both maps below. Then answer the questions that follow.

Map A: Florida
Map B: Northern Florida

18 About how many miles is it from Tampa to Orlando?
75 miles

19 About how many miles is it from Tallahassee to Lake City?
100 miles

20 Which map would you use to find the distance between Bradenton and Gainesville?
Map A

21 About how many miles is it from Melbourne to Ocala on Map A? on Map B?
120 miles; 120 miles

22 Which map would you use if you needed information about both Jacksonville and Key West? Why?
Map A; because both locations are shown on that map

(continued)

Name _____ Date _____

Part Three: Apply What You Have Learned

Directions Complete each of the following activities.

23 CATEGORIZE SOUTHEAST AND GULF ISLANDS (10 points)

Fill in the circle under the island or group of islands that fits each description. Sometimes more than one circle should be filled in.

	Barrier Islands	Puerto Rico	U.S. Virgin Islands	Florida Keys
a. protects the mainland during storms	●	○	○	○
b. People can drive to these islands.	●	○	○	●
c. Most food and water must be imported.	○	○	●	●
d. made of sand, shells, and soil	●	○	○	○
e. the peaks of underwater mountains	○	●	●	○
f. has rain forests and swamps	○	●	●	○
g. located in the tropics	○	●	●	○
h. popular with tourists	●	●	●	●
i. a territory of the United States	○	●	●	○
j. Residents are citizens of the United States.	●	●	●	●

24 ESSAY (10 points)

In a one-paragraph essay, explain why the Southeast and Gulf region is a good location for farming.

Possible response: The fertile Coastal Plain covers more than half of the region. Farmers also find fertile land along broad floodplains and on the Mississippi Delta. As part of the Sun Belt, the region has a long growing season. It also has plentiful rainfall. In addition, the region has many navigable rivers, deep harbors, and two coastlines from which farm products can be shipped to markets. All of these factors make the Southeast and Gulf region a good place for farming.

© Harcourt

ANSWERS

Name _____ Date _____

7 Test

Part One: Test Your Understanding

MULTIPLE CHOICE (4 points each)

Directions Circle the letter of the best answer.

1 Which of the following features is *not* found along the Gulf Coast of the South Central region?
A inlets
B beaches
C marshes
D deserts

2 Who were the first Europeans to claim land in the South Central region?
F the English
G the Spanish
H the French
J the Dutch

3 Why was Oklahoma settled by Europeans much later than the rest of the South Central states?
A The land was less fertile in Oklahoma.
B For many years, only Native Americans were allowed to live there.
C Oklahoma has no navigable rivers for transportation.
D The land in Oklahoma cost more than the land in other parts of the region.

4 How did Texas ranchers get their cattle to markets elsewhere in the country?
F They shipped the cattle on boats down rivers.
G They made the cattle walk the entire way.
H They shipped the cattle on railroads.
J They shipped the cattle on barges from the Gulf of Mexico.

5 What happens in a refinery?
A People build and test equipment for air and space travel.
B People use equipment to turn crude oil into useful products, such as gasoline.
C People dig out the bottoms and sides of waterways.
D People drill crude oil from the ground.

(continued)

Chapter 7 Test   Assessment Program ▪ 45

Name _____ Date _____

6 Large ships can sail into the port of Houston, Texas, because—
F the city is located on the Atlantic Ocean.
G people built a canal linking the city to the Gulf of Mexico.
H people dredged the bayou, connecting the city to the Gulf of Mexico.
J the city is the nation's largest center for oil refining.

7 Which of these industries is *not* a major part of the South Central region's diverse economy?
A service industries
B drilling for oil
C farming and ranching
D coal mining

8 What caused a conflict between the United States and Mexico over their shared border?
F People disagreed about building dams on the Rio Grande.
G The channel of the Rio Grande moved south after floods.
H People in Texas used too much water for irrigation.
J Industries in Mexico were dumping harmful wastes into the Rio Grande.

9 Which of the following is *not* a way people in the United States and Mexico share the Rio Grande?
A They work together to build dams and reservoir projects along the river.
B They share the common border formed by the Rio Grande.
C They follow the same laws to prevent pollution in the river.
D They share the river's waters for irrigation.

IDENTIFICATION (4 points each)

Directions For each group of terms, circle the letter of the term that does *not* belong with the other two.

10 a. crude oil   b. aerospace   **c.** refinery

11 a. inlet   b. bayou   **c.** runoff

12 **a.** petrochemical   b. conflict   c. compromise

13 a. arid   **b.** expedition   c. irrigation

14 **a.** dredge   b. petroleum   c. wealth

15 a. El Chamizal   b. Rio Grande   **c.** Ozark Plateau

(continued)

46 ▪ Assessment Program   Chapter 7 Test

Name _____ Date _____

Part Two: Test Your Skills

RESOLVE CONFLICTS (4 points each) Possible responses are given.

Directions Read each description of a conflict that has occurred in the South Central states. For each, describe the steps people took to resolve the conflict.

16 The Mexican government passed several laws raising taxes in Texas and limiting new settlement there. Many people in Texas thought these laws were unfair.

At first, Texans tried to settle the conflict peacefully by sending Stephen F.

Austin to Mexico to try to convince Mexico's leaders to change the laws. When

those actions did not settle the conflict, however, Texas declared its

independence from Mexico.

17 People in Colorado, New Mexico, Texas, and Mexico all depend on the Rio Grande for irrigation. However, the riverbed was sometimes dry in parts of the Rio Grande valley.

The United States government built dams across the Rio Grande so that all of

the states along the river could share the waters. The United States worked with

Mexico to build additional dams on the river. The United States also agreed that

a certain amount of the Rio Grande's water must reach Mexico.

18 The channel of the Rio Grande moved south after floods. Land that had been part of Mexico was then north of the Rio Grande. People in the United States and Mexico disagreed about who owned that land.

The United States gave El Chamizal back to Mexico, and Mexico gave the

United States some land on the north side of the Rio Grande's original channel.

Both countries agreed that the Rio Grande is their official border. Both countries

also worked together to line the new riverbed with concrete to make sure that the

Rio Grande would not change course again.

(continued)

Chapter 7 Test   Assessment Program ▪ 47

Name _____ Date _____

Part Three: Apply What You Have Learned

Directions Complete each of the following activities.

19 CATEGORIZE FEATURES OF THE SOUTH CENTRAL STATES (18 points)

Use the graphic organizer below to describe the different ways the South Central states make up a region of variety. For each category, write three factors that illustrate the variety of the region. Possible responses are given.

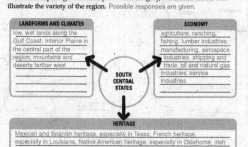

LANDFORMS AND CLIMATES
low, wet lands along the Gulf Coast; Interior Plains in the central part of the region; mountains and deserts farther west

ECONOMY
agriculture, ranching, fishing, lumber industries, manufacturing, aerospace industries, shipping and trade, oil and natural gas industries, service industries

SOUTH CENTRAL STATES

HERITAGE
Mexican and Spanish heritage, especially in Texas; French heritage, especially in Louisiana; Native American heritage, especially in Oklahoma; Irish and Scottish heritage, especially in Arkansas; African American heritage throughout the region

20 ESSAY (10 points)

Many industries in the South Central states depend on natural resources. In a one-paragraph essay, describe some of those industries and the natural resources they use.

Possible response: Much of the South Central region has fertile soil and a long

growing season to produce large crops. In drier parts of the region, people use

the land for ranching. The region's forests support lumber industries and supply

raw materials for manufacturing wood products. The region's waterways supply

fish products and transportation routes for shipping and trade. The region's petro-

leum and natural gas resources are used in oil industries. In addition, the region's

beautiful landscapes and other attractions support a large tourism industry.

48 ▪ Assessment Program   Chapter 7 Test

© Harcourt

ANSWERS

·UNIT·

3 Test

Part One: Test Your Understanding

MULTIPLE CHOICE (2 points each)

Directions Circle the letter of the best answer.

1 What hardships did the early Jamestown colonists face?
A Hurricanes blew in from the coast, destroying their homes.
B They competed and fought with other colonists for land.
(C) Much of the water they found was salty and unhealthy to drink.
D They could not find any fertile soil to grow food.

2 Why did many cities along the Fall Line become centers of trade?
F They were located along deep harbors on Chesapeake Bay.
G Ships could go upstream from the Coastal Plain all the way to the Mississippi River.
H The land around the Fall Line is good for farming.
(J) They connected settlements along the Atlantic Ocean with the new settlements west of the Appalachian Mountains.

3 Which of the following is *not* a way people in the South region use rivers?
A as transportation
B to create electricity
C for irrigation
(D) to produce natural gas

4 Why do businesses often have offices in state capitals?
F State laws require businesses to have offices in state capitals.
G Businesses do not have to pay taxes in state capitals.
(H) Business owners want to be near government leaders and offices that affect their work.
J State capitals are always the largest cities in their states.

5 Why did most early Spanish expeditions come to explore the South region?
A They came in search of religious freedom.
B They came to drill for oil and natural gas.
(C) They came in search of gold and other riches.
D They came to start plantations.

(continued)

Unit 3 Test   Assessment Program ▪ 49

6 How was the United States divided during the Civil War?
F into states that allowed slavery and states that did not allow slavery
(G) into the Confederacy, the Union, and border states
H into agricultural states and manufacturing states
J into territories claimed by the United States and territories claimed by France

7 Food processing and textile manufacturing are industries that—
(A) are related to agriculture.
B are located only along the Gulf Coast.
C need plentiful rainfall and a long growing season.
D rely on the South's nonrenewable resources.

8 Imports are—
(F) goods brought into one country from another country.
G trade among nations.
H goods shipped from one country to another country.
J resources that can be used to manufacture a product.

9 As you go from east to west across the South region—
A the elevation of the land gets lower.
B the cities get larger.
C the states get smaller.
(D) the climate becomes drier.

10 How are the South Central states different from the rest of the South states?
F They border the Gulf of Mexico.
(G) They have desert areas.
H They have several barrier islands off the coast.
J They do not have fertile land.

11 Which of the following events occurred first in the South region?
A English settlers started the Jamestown Colony.
(B) Spanish explorers claimed much of the region.
C The American Civil War was fought.
D The United States purchased the Mississippi River valley from France.

(continued)

50 ▪ Assessment Program   Unit 3 Test

TRUE OR FALSE (2 points each)

Directions Read each of the statements below about the South region. In the space next to each, write T if the statement is true. Write F if the statement is false.

12 T The region has many marshes, swamps, and bayous.
13 F Pioneers had to cross the Rocky Mountains to settle the entire region.
14 T Parts of the region were once claimed by Spain and France.
15 F All of the South states border either the Atlantic Ocean or the Gulf of Mexico.
16 T The region lies in the Sun Belt.
17 F None of the South states lie in the Interior Plains.
18 F The Mississippi River forms the western boundary of the South region.
19 T Tourism is a large industry in all of the South states.

SHORT ANSWER (2 points each)

Directions Write the answer to each question on the lines provided.

20 How did Daniel Boone help people settle parts of the South region?
He helped clear the Wilderness Road through the Cumberland Gap, which allowed people to travel by wagon over the Appalachian Mountains.

21 How do people in the South states use the region's forests to earn a living?
for lumber industries; to manufacture pulp, paper, furniture, and other wood products

22 Why is shipping a large industry in the South states?
because many of the South states border the Atlantic Ocean and the Gulf of Mexico; because most of the South states have navigable rivers that can be used to ship goods to the ocean

23 How did the discovery of oil affect parts of the South region?
Drilling for oil and manufacturing products from oil became large industries in the South; cities grew up near the oil wells.

(continued)

Unit 3 Test   Assessment Program ▪ 51

Part Two: Test Your Skills

COMPARE MAPS WITH DIFFERENT SCALES (2 points each)

Directions Study the two maps on page 53. Then use the maps to answer the following questions.

24 How are the two maps alike?
They both show South Carolina.

25 How are the two maps different?
They use different scales; more details are shown on Map A, and more locations in surrounding states are shown on Map B.

26 Look at the map scales on Map A and Map B. How many miles does one inch represent on each map?
Map A: 1 inch = 60 miles; Map B: 1 inch = 120 miles

27 How many miles is it from Charleston to Myrtle Beach on Map A? on Map B?
about 90 miles; about 90 miles

28 How many miles is it from Atlanta, Georgia, to Greenville, South Carolina? Which map did you use to answer this question?
about 150 miles; Map B

29 How many miles separate the capital of South Carolina and the capital of Georgia? Which map did you use to answer this question? Why?
about 200 miles; Map B; because both of those locations are shown on Map B, but Atlanta is not shown on Map A

30 If you were traveling to South Carolina on vacation, which map would you take with you? Why?
Map A; because more cities and other locations in South Carolina are shown on Map A than are shown on Map B

(continued)

52 ▪ Assessment Program   Unit 3 Test

© Harcourt

ANSWER KEY   **Assessment Program ▪ 131**

ANSWERS

Name _____ Date _____

Map A: South Carolina

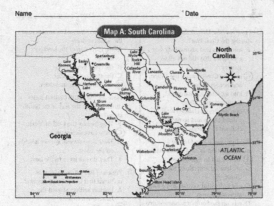

Map B: South Carolina

(continued)

Name _____ Date _____

Part Three: Apply What You Have Learned

Directions Complete each of the following activities.

31 IDENTIFY LOCATIONS ON A MAP (8 points)

Match the description of each place below with the correct letter on the map. Then write the letter in the space provided.

The South

a. __H__ important area for coal mining

b. __E__ the busiest port in the United States

c. __A__ the largest center for oil refining in the United States

d. __B__ the southernmost city in the South states

e. __F__ De Soto was among the first Europeans to cross this river

f. __D__ the most-visited national park in the United States

g. __C__ the center of the national government

h. __G__ the first lasting English settlement in North America

(continued)

Name _____ Date _____

32 IDENTIFY CAUSE AND EFFECT (10 points)

Complete the chart below to identify some of the causes and effects of changes and events that have occurred in the South. Possible answers are given.

CAUSE	→	EFFECT
Many cities were built along the Atlantic and Gulf Coasts or along major rivers.	→	Many cities in the South region are busy ports.
People from many different countries settled in the South region.	→	The South region today has a mix of people and cultures.
Much of the South region has a long growing season and plentiful rainfall.	→	Agriculture is an important industry throughout the South.
The United States and Mexico compromised to settle the conflict over their shared border along the Rio Grande.	→	The Rio Grande is the official border between the United States and Mexico.
People discovered large deposits of coal, oil, and natural gas in the South region.	→	Coal mining, drilling for oil and natural gas, and manufacturing products from oil are large industries in the South.

(continued)

Name _____ Date _____

33 IDENTIFY CAUSE AND EFFECT (12 points)

Listed below are three examples of decisions people have made in the South that changed the place where they lived. Describe two ways in which each of the decisions changed the environment of the South. Possible responses are given.

DECISIONS PEOPLE MADE	EFFECTS ON THE ENVIRONMENT
People decided to build coal mines in Appalachia.	The land eroded because grasses and trees had been removed to mine the coal.
	Parts of Appalachia were destroyed or badly damaged.
People decided to build dams and power plants in the Tennessee River Valley.	Dams created reservoirs and helped control flooding.
	Having a good source of electricity brought more industries and people to the region.
People decided to develop tourism on the Florida Keys.	The islands became more crowded.
	Pollution increased, harming nearby coral reefs.

34 ESSAY (10 points)

The climate of the Sun Belt is generally mild all year long. In a one-paragraph essay, explain how this climate affects the South region.

Possible response: The warm climate allows farmers to raise certain crops that need a long growing season, such as cotton, sugarcane, rice, and citrus fruits. The warm, sunny climate attracts more people and businesses to the region. People can enjoy the South's many tourist attractions year-round. All of these factors have helped the South states become one of the fastest-growing regions in the United States.

© Harcourt

ANSWERS

Individual Performance Task

South Stamps

The first United States postage stamps were issued in 1847. Since then, the United States Postal Service has issued many special postage stamps called commemorative stamps. These stamps often honor people or events from the past that have had a great effect on the United States. Most commemorative stamps include an illustration, the name of the country that issued the stamp, and the value of the stamp. In some cases, the stamp's illustration also contains a brief title or description of what is pictured. If an event is shown, the stamp may also tell the date of the event.

1 Select one of the following topics for your postage stamp, or, with the approval of your teacher, select your own topic.

• The founding of the Jamestown Colony	• The American Civil War
• The Oklahoma land rush	• Islands of the South region
• The Texas war for independence	• Spanish exploration of the South
• Crossing the Appalachian Mountains	• The "Lost Colony" of Roanoke

2 Find information in your textbook and do research on the Internet or in your school's library to learn more about your topic.

3 Make a rough sketch of your stamp on a large sheet of paper. Make sure it contains all the parts of a real postage stamp.

4 Show your sketch to a classmate, and ask whether your design is clear and can be understood.

5 Improve the rough sketch and make any changes that are necessary.

6 Refer to your sketch to make a final copy of your stamp on posterboard.

7 Present and explain your postage stamp to the rest of the class. Then display your stamp in the classroom for others to enjoy.

Group Performance Task

Industry Report

Many of the major industries in the South have been an important part of the region's economy since colonial days. However, each of those industries has changed in many ways over time. In this task your group will create a presentation explaining the history of an industry in the South.

1 As a group, select one of the following industries to be the subject of your presentation, or, with the approval of your teacher, select your own topic.

• Agriculture	• Cattle ranching
• Coal mining	• Hydroelectric power
• Oil production	• Shipping and trade
• Tourism	• High-tech industries

2 Assign each member of your group a different aspect of the industry to research. Some aspects to consider are the history of the industry in the region; where in the region the industry is located today; and resources the industry uses.

3 Use your textbook, the Internet, and library resources to learn more about your topic. Each member of your group should try to find information that matches the aspect of the industry he or she is assigned.

4 As a group, make an outline of the information you will include in your presentation. Create illustrations, maps, graphs, or time lines to make the information easier to understand. You may also want to use photographs, artifacts, and quotations in your presentation.

5 Practice the presentation. Time yourselves with a watch to determine how long the presentation will take. It should be no longer than five minutes. All members of the group should prepare notes to help with their parts of the presentation.

6 Rehearse your presentation at least once. Be sure to use your illustrations, graphs, or other props in your rehearsal. Everyone in your group should give part of the presentation.

7 Give your industry presentation to the rest of the class. Then hold a short question-and-answer session about the industry.

INDIVIDUAL PERFORMANCE TASK

Score 4	Score 3	Score 2	Score 1
• Designs show excellent creativity.	• Designs show some creativity.	• Designs show little creativity.	• Designs show no creativity.
• Details are well researched.	• Details are researched.	• Details reflect little research.	• Details show no evidence of research.
• Stamps are very informative.	• Stamps are informative.	• Stamps are not very informative.	• Stamps are not informative.

GROUP PERFORMANCE TASK

Score 4	Score 3	Score 2	Score 1
• Presentation shows excellent creativity.	• Presentation shows some creativity.	• Presentation shows little creativity.	• Presentation shows no creativity.
• Presentation is very well researched and organized.	• Presentation is researched and organized.	• Presentation is poorly researched and organized.	• Presentation is not researched or organized.
• Presentation is very informative.	• Presentation is informative.	• Presentation is not very informative.	• Presentation is not informative.

ANSWERS

Name _____ Date _____

8 Test

Part One: Test Your Understanding

MULTIPLE CHOICE (3 points each)

Directions Circle the letter of the best answer.

1 Why did Marquette and Joliet explore the Great Lakes region?
A to build trading posts along rivers
(B) to find and explore the Mississippi River
C to search for gold and silver
D to find a water route between Canada and the United States

2 Fighting over ownership of the Ohio River valley led to what war?
F the American Revolution
(G) the French and Indian War
H the American Civil War
J the War of 1812

3 Which of the following does *not* describe the Northwest Territory?
A It included the lands west of Pennsylvania and east of the Mississippi River.
(B) It was the first area in which the French built settlements in North America.
C It was divided into townships and sold to settlers.
D It included the lands north of the Ohio River and south of the Great Lakes.

4 Why did the United States decide to survey the Northwest Territory?
(F) to better plan for the settlement of the territory
G to set up a plan for governing the territory
H to describe the steps by which new states would be formed in the territory
J to plan where to locate capital cities in the territory

5 What caused the Great Lakes to form?
(A) glaciers
B floods
C earthquakes
D hurricanes

(continued)

Chapter 8 Test   Assessment Program ■ 59

Name _____ Date _____

6 The Illinois Waterway and the Illinois River connect Lake Michigan with—
F Lake Huron.
(G) the Mississippi River.
H Lake Superior.
J the Ohio River.

7 Why were steel mills built along the Great Lakes?
A The climate in the area is good for making steel.
B No other region in the United States has coal.
(C) Both iron ore and coal were found in nearby states.
D There was a large automobile industry in the region.

8 Most manufactured goods today are—
F made by hand.
(G) made on assembly lines.
H made by robots.
J made in the Great Lakes states.

9 Which of these boats cannot travel upstream against a river's current?
(A) flatboat
B keelboat
C steamboat
D barge

COMPLETION (3 points each)

Directions Fill in the blanks with terms from the list to complete the sentence. You will not use one term.

10 In the Northwest Territory, one section in each _____township_____ was set aside for a school.

11 An _____ordinance_____ is a set of laws.

12 Settlers on the _____frontier_____ were often surrounded by wilderness.

13 _____Ore_____ is rock that contains one or more kinds of minerals.

14 The world's first _____skyscraper_____ was built in Chicago in 1885.

15 Goods shipped on rivers are often called _____freight_____

16 A _____barge_____ is a flat-bottomed boat used mostly on rivers and other inland waterways.

ore
frontier
skyscraper
ordinance
barge
paddy
township
freight

(continued)

60 ■ Assessment Program   Chapter 8 Test

Name _____ Date _____

Part Two: Test Your Skills

MAKE A THOUGHTFUL DECISION (4 points each)   Possible responses are given.

Directions Read each decision people have made in the history of the Great Lakes states. For each, write one consequence of that decision.

17 In 1673 French leaders in what is today Canada decided to send an expedition to explore the areas south of the Great Lakes.
Many French traders moved to the Great Lakes region and set up trading posts that grew into towns and cities over time.

18 The United States government decided to sell land in the Northwest Territory for as little as a dollar per acre.
Thousands of settlers moved to the Northwest Territory in hopes of buying their own land for the first time.

19 Automobile manufacturers decided to use mass production in their factories.
Automobiles were produced much faster and less expensively, and the automobile industry grew rapidly in the Great Lakes states.

20 People decided to build locks and dams along the Mississippi River in the Great Lakes region.
Navigation was improved on the Mississippi River, especially the route to Minneapolis, Minnesota. Trade and industries grew rapidly along the Mississippi River in the Great Lakes region.

(continued)

Chapter 8 Test   Assessment Program ■ 61

Name _____ Date _____

Part Three: Apply What You Have Learned

Directions Complete each of the following activities.

21 SUMMARIZE INFORMATION ABOUT RIVERS (26 points)

Complete the chart below to summarize information about some major rivers around the world.

RIVER	CONTINENT	USES
Mississippi River	North America	migration route for settlers traveling west; transportation, shipping, and trade; site of many large cities and industries
Nile River	Africa	source of fresh water, irrigation, and hydroelectric power
Chang Jiang	Asia	shipping; irrigation, especially for rice paddies; site of many large cities and industries
Ganges River	Asia	transportation; water for farming and drinking; a holy site for Hindus
Amazon River	South America	transportation; supports vegetation in the rain forest
Rhine River	Europe	major shipping route for industries throughout Europe to reach an ocean port

22 ESSAY (10 points)

Mass production and the assembly line were two important developments in American industry. In a one-paragraph essay, explain what they are and why they are important.
Possible response: Mass production means making many things that are all alike and can be made quickly and cheaply using machines. An assembly line is a line of workers along which a product moves as it is put together one step at a time. These developments helped industries make products faster and more cheaply so that more people could afford to buy them.

62 ■ Assessment Program   Chapter 8 Test

© Harcourt

ANSWERS

·CHAPTER·

Name _____ Date _____

9 Test

Part One: Test Your Understanding

MULTIPLE CHOICE (4 points each)

Directions Circle the letter of the best answer.

1 Which of the following statements about the Plains region is *not* true?
A The French were the first Europeans to explore the Plains region.
B The Plains region includes both the Central Plains and the Great Plains.
C Miles of prairie grasses once covered the Plains region.
(D) Europeans settled in the Plains region before they settled in the Great Lakes region.

2 Why did the government pass the Homestead Act in 1862?
(F) to encourage people to settle on the Great Plains
G to set aside lands on the Great Plains for Native Americans
H to encourage railroad companies to build tracks across the Great Plains
J to clear more land for wheat farmers on the Great Plains

3 Why is prairie soil naturally very fertile?
A There is little precipitation on the prairies.
(B) When the prairie grasses die, they leave behind matter that enriches the soil.
C Farmers add fertilizers to the soil.
D When the Missouri River floods each year, it leaves behind rich silt.

4 What did most pioneers on the Great Plains use to build their homes?
(F) sod
G logs
H buffalo skins
J bricks

5 Where did many Sioux settle in the Plains region during the 1600s?
A in Wisconsin and Minnesota
B in Missouri and Iowa
C in Kansas and Nebraska
(D) in North Dakota and South Dakota

Chapter 9 Test

Assessment Program ■ 63

Name _____ Date _____

6 What crop changed farming on the Great Plains?
F dent corn
G sunflowers
(H) winter wheat
J rye grass

7 Why did meat packing become a major industry in the Plains states?
(A) because cattle and hogs are raised in the region
B because Texas ranchers drove their cattle to the Plains states
C because there is a low demand for meat in other regions
D because farmers in the region produce dent corn to feed the cattle

8 A fall in a demand for a good or service often leads to a fall in—
F temperature.
(G) supply.
H urbanization.
J free enterprise.

9 How are most of the world's plains used?
A for shipping
B for manufacturing
C for mining
(D) for agriculture

TRUE OR FALSE (4 points each)

Directions Read each of the following statements about the Plains states. In the space next to each, write *T* if the statement is true or *F* if the statement is false.

10 __F__ All of the Plains states lie mostly in the Great Plains.

11 __T__ The Sioux depended on buffalo for many of their needs.

12 __F__ More people live on farms today than ever before.

13 __T__ The Plains states, like all of the United States, have a free enterprise economy.

14 __T__ For many years, corn and wheat were the two largest crops in the Plains region.

15 __T__ Most early settlers in the Plains region had to be self-sufficient.

(continued)

64 ■ Assessment Program

Chapter 9 Test

Name _____ Date _____

Part Two: Test Your Skills

READ A DOUBLE-BAR GRAPH (4 points each)

Directions The double-bar graph below shows the numbers of people living in urban and rural regions in each of the Plains states. Use the bar graph to answer the questions that follow.

16 In which Plains states do more than 1 million people live in rural regions?
Iowa and Missouri

Urban and Rural Populations in the Plains States

SOURCE: U.S. Census Bureau

17 How do the urban and rural populations of Nebraska compare?
Possible response: About twice as many people in Nebraska live in urban regions as live in rural regions.

18 Do more people in the Plains states live in urban or rural regions?
urban regions

19 Which Plains state has the highest total population? How can you tell from this double-bar graph?
Missouri; both its urban and its rural population bars are the highest on the graph.

20 In which Plains state are the urban and rural population numbers closer, Kansas or South Dakota?
South Dakota

(continued)

Chapter 9 Test

Assessment Program ■ 65

Name _____ Date _____

Part Three: Apply What You Have Learned

Directions Complete each of the following activities.

21 COMPARE PLAINS REGIONS (10 points) Possible responses are given.

The Interior Plains in the United States and the Pampas in Argentina are alike in many ways. Describe five ways in which both areas are the same.

a. The Interior Plains and the Pampas both have mostly flat land.

b. Both have very rich soil.

c. The west is drier than the east in both regions.

d. Wheat and corn are leading crops in both regions.

e. Cattle ranching is a major industry in both regions.

22 ESSAY (10 points)

Farming methods and technology are constantly changing. In a one-paragraph essay, describe some of the changes that have affected farming in the United States over the years.

Possible response: New inventions such as iron plows, reapers, threshers, and combines have allowed farmers to grow and harvest crops faster and more easily. Other technologies such as fertilizers, airplanes, computers, and chemicals to kill weeds and insects have also helped farmers grow larger crops. All of these changes have helped farmers raise more crops on each acre of land and plant crops on more land. As a result, most farms in the United States today are much larger than they were in the past, require fewer workers, and produce larger crops.

66 ■ Assessment Program

Chapter 9 Test

© Harcourt

ANSWERS

Name _____ Date _____

4 Test

Part One: Test Your Understanding

MULTIPLE CHOICE (2 points each)

Directions Circle the letter of the best answer.

1 Why are the six Great Lakes states grouped into one region?
A because they are all major steel-producing states
B because each of those states borders at least one of the Great Lakes
C because the Great Lakes are the most important means of transportation for all of those states
D because they are the only states in the United States that border the Great Lakes

2 One reason Detroit, Michigan, became a center for the automobile industry was that—
F it was located in the center of the Middle West region.
G there were many steel mills in Detroit to supply automobile manufacturers.
H rivers and lakes made it easy to ship steel and automobiles in and out of Detroit.
J the Mesabi Range, which holds large iron ore deposits, is located next to Detroit.

3 What made mass production of automobiles and other products possible?
A navigable rivers
B assembly lines
C natural resources
D hydroelectric power

4 Which of these is the longest river in the United States?
F the Mississippi River
G the Detroit River
H the Ohio River
J the Missouri River

5 What European country was the first to claim most of both the Great Lakes region and the Plains region?
A Holland
B England
C Spain
D France

(continued)

Name _____ Date _____

6 When did the Plains region become part of the United States?
F soon after the American Revolution ended in 1783
G as part of the Louisiana Purchase of 1803
H as part of the Homestead Act passed in 1862
J as part of the Northwest Ordinance passed in 1787

7 Which of these is the main difference between the Central Plains and the Great Plains?
A More people live on the Great Plains.
B More corn is grown on the Great Plains.
C The Central Plains get more precipitation.
D The Central Plains are flatter and have fewer trees.

8 Which of these statements is *not* true of railroads in the Middle West?
F They helped the ranching industry grow in the region.
G Many cities grew up along their tracks.
H They provided a way for settlers to move to the region.
J They ended the need for the long Texas cattle drives.

9 Which of these storms is not likely to happen on the Interior Plains?
A a blizzard
B a tornado
C a hurricane
D a hailstorm

10 Which of the following is *not* a leading crop of the Middle West?
F corn
G wheat
H peanuts
J soybeans

11 Which of these is always true for plains regions?
A Plains regions have fewer large cities than other regions.
B Plains regions have mostly flat land.
C Soil in plains regions is always fertile.
D Cattle ranching is always a large industry on plains.

(continued)

Name _____ Date _____

IDENTIFICATION (2 points each)

Directions For each group of terms, circle the letter of the term that does *not* belong with the other two.

12 a. township   b. survey   **c.** ore
13 a. adapt   **b.** ordinance   c. tepee
14 a. mass production   **b.** paddy   c. assembly line
15 **a.** skyscraper   b. supply   c. demand
16 a. station   b. estancia   **c.** consumer
17 a. entrepreneur   b. free enterprise   **c.** frontier
18 a. sod   **b.** urbanization   c. prairie

(continued)

Name _____ Date _____

SHORT ANSWER (2 points each)

Directions Write the answer to each question on the lines provided.

19 Why did most early settlers in the Middle West have to be self-sufficient?
because their homes on the frontier were often a long way from towns or neighbors

20 Why do many people choose to live along rivers and lakes?
because rivers and lakes provide transportation and supply fresh water for drinking, washing, and growing crops; rivers also can be used to supply energy

21 In the past, why was corn the leading crop on the Central Plains while wheat was the leading crop on the Great Plains?
because corn grew well in the wetter climate of the Central Plains, while wheat can grow in drier climates such as that of the Great Plains

22 How does our free enterprise economy offer choices to consumers?
Consumers are free to choose what products and services to buy or not to buy.

23 Why is urbanization happening rapidly in the Middle West?
Fewer people are needed to work on farms today than in the past, and many manufacturing and service jobs are located in cities.

(continued)

ANSWERS

Part Two: Test Your Skills

READ A CULTURAL MAP (2 points each)

Directions As Europeans settled in the Americas over time, they brought their different cultures with them, including their languages. The cultural map on page 72 shows where in the Americas those languages are spoken today. Use the map to answer the following questions.

24. What language is spoken on most of the North American continent?

   English

25. What languages are spoken in Central America?

   Spanish and American Indian languages

26. What is the largest area of the Americas in which French is spoken?

   eastern Canada

27. How does the map show you that people from Portugal settled parts of the eastern coast of South America?

   because the map shows that Portuguese is spoken there

28. How does the map show you that Spain had settlements in both North America and South America?

   because Spanish is spoken on both continents

29. What on the map supports the idea that few Europeans settled in the inland areas of northern South America?

   Many people in those areas speak American Indian languages instead of European

   languages.

30. Which of the five European languages named in the map key is spoken least in the Americas today?

   Dutch

(continued)

Present-Day Languages of the Americas

Key:
- Spanish
- Portuguese
- English
- French
- Dutch
- American Indian languages

(continued)

Part Three: Apply What You Have Learned

Directions Complete each of the following activities.

31. **CATEGORIZE RESOURCES AND INDUSTRIES** (10 points)

For each resource or product of the Middle West in the table below, name an industry in that region that uses it. Possible responses are given.

RESOURCE OR PRODUCT	INDUSTRY
Wheat crops	flour mills
Cattle	meat packing
Steel	automobile manufacturing
Waterways	shipping and trade
Iron ore	steel mills

32. **CATEGORIZE CITIES IN THE MIDDLE WEST** (8 points)

Many cities in the Middle West have grown up along waterways. For each city listed below, write **GL** if it grew up along the Great Lakes. Write **MS** if the city grew up along the Mississippi River system.

a. _GL_ Chicago, Illinois   e. _MS_ Minneapolis, Minnesota

b. _MS_ St. Louis, Missouri   f. _MS_ Dubuque, Iowa

c. _GL_ Cleveland, Ohio   g. _GL_ Detroit, Michigan

d. _GL_ Milwaukee, Wisconsin   h. _MS_ Kansas City, Kansas

(continued)

---

33. **DESCRIBE INTERDEPENDENCE IN THE MIDDLE WEST** (8 points)

People who live in cities and on farms and ranches in the Middle West depend on one another. List three ways farmers and ranchers depend on city dwellers and three ways city dwellers depend on farmers and ranchers. Possible responses are given.

FARMERS AND RANCHERS DEPEND ON CITY DWELLERS	CITY DWELLERS DEPEND ON FARMERS AND RANCHERS
Farmers and ranchers depend on city dwellers to have customers to sell their products to. They need goods manufactured in cities, such as processed foods, computers, and gasoline. They also depend on cities for the machinery and chemicals they need to run their farms and ranches.	City dwellers depend on farmers and ranchers for food. They also depend on farmers and ranchers for raw materials to manufacture products, such as flour and cereals, in city factories. Some city factories also depend on farmers to buy their products, such as farm machinery and fertilizers.

34. **SEQUENCE RIVER TRANSPORTATION** (4 points)

In this unit you read about four types of river transportation in the United States—barges, flatboats, steamboats, and keelboats. In the chart below, place them in the correct order, from the first introduced to the last introduced.

FIRST			LAST
flatboats	keelboats	steamboats	barges

35. **ESSAY** (10 points)

In a one-paragraph essay, describe how people have adapted to the environment of the Interior Plains over time.

Possible response: The Sioux adapted by using horses to hunt buffalo and by

living in tepees. Early settlers adapted by using sod to build their houses and being

self-sufficient. Early farmers adapted by growing the crops that did well in the

different climates of the Interior Plains—corn in the Central Plains and winter

wheat in the Great Plains. Today, many industries have adapted by supplying

what people in the Interior Plains demand, such as farm equipment, fertilizers,

and flour mills.

© Harcourt

ANSWERS

Individual Performance Task

Supplying Demands

Most businesses that succeed meet a demand, or supply something that many people are willing to pay for. In the Middle West region, for example, flour mills met the demand for grinding winter wheat, while Joseph McCoy's stockyard in Abilene, Kansas, supplied a way to ship cattle to eastern markets. In many ways, supply and demand are the secret to success in business. For this task you will imagine you are writing a plan for a business you want to start in your community.

❶ Brainstorm ideas for your business. Think about the businesses that already exist in your community. Are there any products or services not available in your community that you think people would want, such as bicycle repairs, computer services, or party supplies? Consider your own interests, too, since you will most likely have to work long hours to start your business. Whatever you choose should be something you enjoy or care about.

❷ Choose your business. Then use the Internet or library resources to gather information about that kind of business. Research similar businesses in your community or elsewhere. You may wish to conduct a survey in your community to ask people if your service or product is something people want.

❸ Write a business plan describing what good or service you will supply and what demand it will meet. Explain why you think your business will be a success in your community. You may wish to add graphs, tables, maps, or illustrations to your plan to make the information clearer and more interesting.

❹ Present your business plan to the class. Then ask their opinions about whether they think your business is a good idea for your community.

Group Performance Task

Eyewitness News

In a television news story, a reporter usually talks to one or more people who have taken part in an event. Most news stories have an introduction, one or more interviews, and a conclusion. In this task, your group will imagine they are traveling back in time to cover a historical event. You will prepare a news story as though it will be broadcast on a television news program.

❶ Select one of these topics for a news story or, with the approval of your teacher, select your own topic. Decide which role each member of your group will take.

TOPIC	ROLES
Life in a Sioux community in the 1700s	a reporter, a Sioux chief, a Great Plains settler, members of a Sioux family
Cattle ranching in the 1800s	a reporter, Joseph McCoy, a railroad worker, a cowhand on the cattle drives
The Dust Bowl	a reporter, a farmer on the Great Plains, a meteorologist, a soil erosion expert
The completion of Mount Rushmore	a reporter, one of the first visitors, a park ranger
The automobile industry along the Great Lakes	a reporter, Henry Ford, an automobile factory worker, a steel mill owner

❷ Use your textbook and library resources to learn more about your topic. Each member of your group should try to find information that matches his or her role.

❸ As a group, make an outline of the questions the reporter will ask and the answers that the others will give. Each person in the group should have specific things to say.

❹ Practice the news story. Time yourselves with a watch to determine how long the story will take. It should be no longer than five minutes. All members of the group should prepare notes to help with their parts of the presentation.

❺ Present the news story to the rest of the class. Everyone in the group should act as though they are on a live television program.

INDIVIDUAL PERFORMANCE TASK

Score 4	Score 3	Score 2	Score 1
• Main ideas are well supported with details. • Details are well researched and accurate. • Overall presentation is very creative, informative, and practical.	• Main ideas are supported with details. • Details are researched and accurate. • Overall presentation is creative, informative, and practical.	• Few main ideas are supported with details. • Few details are researched or accurate. • Overall presentation adds little to the information and is not very practical.	• Main ideas are not supported with details. • Details are not well researched or accurate. • Overall presentation shows little or no effort at communicating information, and the plan is not practical.

GROUP PERFORMANCE TASK

Score 4	Score 3	Score 2	Score 1
• Main ideas are well supported with details. • Details are well researched and accurate. • Presentation is well organized and very informative.	• Main ideas are supported with details. • Details are researched and accurate. • Presentation is organized and informative.	• Few main ideas are supported with details. • Few details are researched or accurate. • Presentation is not well organized and gives little insight into the topic.	• Main ideas are not supported with details. • Details are not well researched or accurate. • Presentation is unorganized and gives no insight into the topic.

ANSWERS

Name _____ Date _____

10 Test

Part One: Test Your Understanding

MULTIPLE CHOICE (4 points each)

Directions Circle the letter of the best answer.

1. Which of the following is *not* an area that Lewis and Clark explored?
   A the Rocky Mountains
   B the Great Plains
   C the Pacific Coast
   D the Mississippi Delta

2. The Continental Divide is—
   F an imaginary line that circles Earth halfway between the North Pole and the South Pole.
   G an imaginary line that runs north to south along the peaks of the Rocky Mountains.
   H an imaginary line that divides Earth into the Eastern Hemisphere and the Western Hemisphere.
   J an imaginary line that runs east to west across North America from the Atlantic Ocean to the Pacific Ocean.

3. Which of the following is the main reason the first Mormon settlers moved to the Mountain region?
   A to mine gold and silver
   B for the right to vote
   C to start cattle ranches
   D for religious freedom

4. In mountain regions, satellites have improved—
   F transportation.
   G international trade.
   H weather conditions.
   J communication.

5. Why do no trees grow above the timberline?
   A because temperatures at that elevation are too cold for trees to grow
   B because precipitation levels are too high at that elevation
   C because forest fires spread quickly at that elevation
   D because less sunlight reaches places at that elevation

(continued)

Chapter 10 Test   Assessment Program ▪ 77

Name _____ Date _____

6. Which of the following natural resources found in the Mountain states does *not* supply energy?
   F gold
   G coal
   H natural gas
   J uranium

7. How do most people earn a living in the Mountain states today?
   A in mining industries
   B in manufacturing industries
   C in service industries
   D in agricultural industries

8. Which of these mountain ranges has the highest mountain peak in the world?
   F the Alps
   G the Himalayas
   H the Andes
   J the Atlas

9. Trading one kind of good for another without using money is called—
   A importing.
   B bartering.
   C irrigating.
   D exporting.

MATCHING (4 points each)

Directions Match each term at the left with the location at the right that best relates to the term. Then write the correct letter in the space provided. One location will match more than one term.

	Term		Location
10	C	boomtown	A. South Pass
11	A	wagon train	B. Yellowstone National Park
12	E	suffrage	C. Denver, Colorado
13	B	geyser	D. Andes Mountains
14	B	public land	E. Wyoming
15	D	terrace	

(continued)

78 ▪ Assessment Program   Chapter 10 Test

Name _____ Date _____

Part Two: Test Your Skills

READ A CUTAWAY DIAGRAM (3 points each)

Directions Use the cutaway diagram of an underground coal mine below to answer the questions that follow.

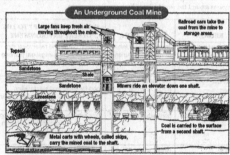

An Underground Coal Mine

16. What materials cover the coal buried underground?
    topsoil, sandstone, shale, and limestone

17. What keeps fresh air moving throughout the coal mine?
    large fans located at the top of each shaft

18. How do miners get into the coal mine?
    They ride an elevator down one of the shafts.

19. How is the coal moved from the mine to storage areas?
    by railroad cars

20. Why are there always two shafts in an underground coal mine?
    One shaft is for an elevator for carrying people; the other is used to remove the coal from the mine.

(continued)

Chapter 10 Test   Assessment Program ▪ 79

Name _____ Date _____

Part Three: Apply What You Have Learned

Directions Complete each of the following activities.

21. **SOLVE PROBLEMS** (15 points)
    In the chart below are problems faced by people living in different mountain regions around the world. Give one solution people have found for each problem.

PROBLEM	SOLUTION
The steep land of the Rocky Mountains is not well suited for building large cities.	Possible response: People built cities in valleys between the Rocky Mountains and on plateaus and plains to the east and west of the mountains.
It is difficult to grow crops in the arid parts of the Mountain states and the areas south of the Atlas Mountains.	Possible response: People use irrigation to grow crops in those areas.
It is impossible to build roads and railroads in many parts of the Himalayas.	Possible response: Many people in the Himalayas rely on yaks for transportation.
Heavy snowfalls in the Alps can damage houses.	Possible response: People build steep-sloped roofs on their homes so that heavy snowfall slides off and does not damage the houses.
It is difficult to farm the steep land in the Andes Mountains.	Possible response: People build terraces into the hillsides to have enough flat land to grow crops.

22. **ESSAY** (10 points)
    In a one-paragraph essay, describe how the Rocky Mountains have affected travel in the Mountain states over the years.

    Possible response: In the past, the Rocky Mountains were a barrier to travel.

    People had to walk or use horses to travel the narrow, steep trails. With the

    discovery of the South Pass, people could use wagons to travel over the

    mountains. After railroads were built, travel greatly improved. Today, people
    can use modern highways and railroads and fly in airplanes, but weather can still
    affect travel in the Mountain states.

80 ▪ Assessment Program   Chapter 10 Test

© Harcourt

ANSWERS

Name _____ Date _____

11 Test

Part One: Test Your Understanding

MULTIPLE CHOICE (4 points each)

Directions Circle the letter of the best answer.

1 Who led one of the first expeditions into the Southwest Desert region?
A Meriwether Lewis and William Clark
B Hernando de Soto
Ⓒ Francisco Vásquez de Coronado
D Ponce de León

2 Which of the following physical features is *not* found in the Southwest Desert region?
F canyons
G mesas
Ⓗ coastal plains
J deserts

3 What did the Anasazi use to build their homes?
A wood
B sod
C buffalo skins
Ⓓ adobe

4 What city was built to be the capital of Spanish New Mexico?
F Phoenix
Ⓖ Santa Fe
H Las Vegas
J Albuquerque

5 Why are natural sources of fresh water scarce in the Southwest Desert states?
A because people use too much groundwater
Ⓑ because the region lies in the rain shadow of the western mountains
C because most of the fresh water is used to irrigate farmland
D because cloudbursts drop only small amounts of rain

6 Which of the following is *not* a way that people in the Southwest Desert states are working to conserve water resources?
F creating water management areas
G using rocks, sand, and desert plants in gardens
Ⓗ passing laws that forbid people from moving to the region
J recycling water in artificial lakes and waterfalls

(continued)

Name _____ Date _____

7 What features do all deserts have in common?
A a hot climate
Ⓑ a dry climate
C sand dunes
D flat, level land

8 Which of these statements about oases is true?
Ⓕ Most of the water at an oasis comes from underground springs.
G Irrigation is not possible in the loose sand at oases.
H An oasis is one of the driest places on Earth.
J Oases are formed by dams holding back water.

COMPLETION (4 points each)

Directions Fill in the blank with the correct term from the list to complete each sentence. You will not use every term.

9 A small steep hill of rock with a flat top is called a ____butte____.

10 In a ____mission____ early Spanish settlers taught Native Americans about Christianity.

11 On a ____reservation____ Native Americans govern themselves.

12 An ____aqueduct____ carries water from reservoirs to places where it is needed.

13 A ____migrant worker____ moves from farm to farm with the seasons, harvesting crops.

14 A ____sand dune____ is formed as blowing sand forms hill-like mounds.

15 Negev farmers build plastic greenhouses over fields to prevent ____evaporation____.

aqueduct
butte
evaporation
migrant worker
mission
nomad
reservation
sand dune

(continued)

Name _____ Date _____

Part Two: Test Your Skills

PREDICT A LIKELY OUTCOME (3 points each)

Directions Predict the likely outcome in each case below based on the information given. Possible responses are given.

16 About 1,000 years ago, the Anasazi began settling in Chaco Canyon in what is today New Mexico. They used irrigation to grow corn and other foods. During the 1100s, the Chaco Canyon area experienced decades of terrible droughts. What would have been the likely outcome for the Anasazi settlements there?
The Anasazi would not be able to grow enough food; they would abandon their settlements in Chaco Canyon.

17 Spanish settlers from Mexico brought the first cattle into what is now the United States. Over time, some of those cattle wandered away, became wild, and spread across the region. Predict the effect this would have on the economy of the Southwest Desert states.
Ranching would become an important part of the economy in the Southwest Desert states.

18 Over the years, many people from Mexico have immigrated to the Southwest Desert region. Predict how this might affect the cultural heritage of the Southwest Desert states.
Many people in the region would have Mexican ancestors, speak Spanish, and observe Mexican holidays and traditions.

19 People have built dams and reservoir projects in the Southwest Desert region to produce a steady supply of water and electricity. What effect might this have on the population there?
The population of the Southwest Desert states would greatly increase.

20 Many Southwest Desert states have passed laws against building new artificial lakes and waterfalls. They have also given awards to people who use rocks, sand, and desert plants in their gardens instead of grass. How do you think this will affect the Southwest Desert states in the future?
People will conserve more water resources.

(continued)

Name _____ Date _____

Part Three: Apply What You Have Learned

Directions Complete each of the following activities.

21 COMPARE DESERTS AROUND THE WORLD (15 points)
Fill in the missing information in the table below to compare some major desert regions around the world. Possible responses are given.

DESERT REGION	LOCATION	HOW PEOPLE ADAPT TO THE DESERT ENVIRONMENT
Southwest Desert States	southwestern United States; North America	building dams and reservoirs; digging wells; using irrigation; planting desert gardens instead of grass
Atacama Desert	the Pacific Coast of South America, stretching from Peru to Chile	building irrigation projects to grow food for mine workers; building dams to supply hydroelectric power
Sahara	northern Africa	living and farming in oases; herding sheep, goats, and camels between oases; using camels for transportation
Negev	Israel, where Africa and Asia meet	building irrigation projects; storing rain water in tanks; building plastic greenhouses over fields; recycling wastewater; using desalinization

22 ESSAY (10 points)
As the population of the Southwest Desert states continues to grow, the region will need more and more water. In a one-paragraph essay, tell how people in the Southwest Desert states get water today.
Possible response: People in the Southwest Desert states get water from rivers or from reservoirs formed by dams built across rivers. They also pump groundwater from wells. Aqueducts, canals, and pipelines carry water from those sources to the places where people live.

ANSWERS

Name _____ Date _____

12 Test

Part One: Test Your Understanding
MULTIPLE CHOICE (4 points each)

Directions Circle the letter of the best answer.

1 Where did many of the first pioneers settle in the Pacific region?
(A) in the Oregon Country
B in Alaska
C in the Sierra Nevada
D in Death Valley

2 Boomtowns in the Pacific region often sprang up because of—
F locations near important crossroads.
(G) the discovery of gold.
H dam and reservoir projects.
J the discovery of oil.

3 What form of communication replaced the Pony Express?
A telephones
B computers
(C) telegraphs
D fax machines

4 Most of the labor on the first transcontinental railroad was done by—
F Native Americans.
G slaves.
(H) immigrants.
J miners.

5 Which of the following statements is *not* true of the Pacific region?
A It has the top farming and manufacturing state in the United States.
B It has the highest and lowest points in the United States.
(C) It has the largest city and megalopolis in the United States.
D It has the wettest and driest places in the United States.

6 What causes an earthquake?
F A tropical storm forms off the Pacific Coast.
G Hot gases, ash, and lava pour out from a crater.
H The surrounding Pacific winds blow moisture over the land.
(J) Layers of rock deep inside Earth move and crack.

(continued)

Chapter 12 Test   Assessment Program ▪ 85

Name _____ Date _____

7 Which of these is an important industry in the Pacific Northwest?
A refining oil
B gold mining
C car manufacturing
(D) cutting lumber

8 Why do people live on only seven of the Hawaiian Islands?
F because transporting raw materials and finished products to and from the other islands is too expensive
G because the other islands have active volcanoes
H because the other islands are not important crossroads
(J) because the other islands are too small or windy, or have no fresh water

9 What is the smallest ocean in the world?
(A) the Arctic Ocean
B the Atlantic Ocean
C the Indian Ocean
D the Pacific Ocean

10 Which of the following is *not* true of most Pacific Rim countries?
F They all share the common border of the Pacific Ocean.
G They frequently experience earthquakes.
(H) They are all islands or groups of islands.
J They have many volcanoes.

MATCHING (4 points each)

Directions Match each term on the right with its meaning. Then write the correct letter in the space provided.

	Meaning	Term
11 __B__	a gold seeker who arrived in California in the mid-1800s	A. ecosystem
12 __C__	a narrow inlet of the ocean between cliffs	B. forty-niner
13 __A__	the relationship between living things and the nonliving environment	C. fjord
14 __F__	low-lying lands where the water level is always near or above the surface of the land	D. monarch
15 __D__	a king or queen	E. produce
16 __E__	fresh fruits and vegetables	F. wetlands

(continued)

86 ▪ Assessment Program   Chapter 12 Test

Name _____ Date _____

Part Two: Test Your Skills
ACT AS A RESPONSIBLE CITIZEN (3 points each)

Directions For each topic below, list two ways that you could act as a responsible citizen. Possible responses are given.

17 Protecting the environment
cleaning up litter and not littering; volunteering in environmental groups;
conserving resources; planting trees and other natural vegetation; working for
laws that limit pollution

18 Conserving natural resources
recycling products; using fewer resources; using public transportation, walking,
or riding a bike more often; planting trees and other natural vegetation

19 Helping people in your community
taking food to needy families; donating clothing and other goods to
organizations that help people in need; getting to know your neighbors;
volunteering in youth centers or retirement homes

20 Learning about your community, state, and country
studying in school; reading newspapers; watching news programs;
attending speeches, lectures, and demonstrations

(continued)

Chapter 12 Test   Assessment Program ▪ 87

Name _____ Date _____

Part Three: Apply What You Have Learned

Directions Complete each of the following activities.

21 COMPARE AND CONTRAST PACIFIC ISLANDS (8 points)

Hawaii, Guam, and American Samoa are all located in the Pacific Ocean. Use the Venn diagram below to list two ways in which they are the same and one way in which they are different. Possible responses are given.

Hawaii	Both	Guam and American Samoa
a state	warm climate Pacific Ocean islands mountains formed by volcanoes mix of cultures Polynesian ancestors tourism military bases service industries food processing fishing	a territory

22 LIST PHYSICAL FEATURES (6 points)
List six physical features that are found in the Pacific states.
Possible responses include mountains, valleys, deserts, rain forests, plateaus,
islands, volcanoes, coasts, bays, and fjords.

23 ESSAY (10 points)
In a one-paragraph essay, describe how tourism plays an important role in the economy of the Pacific states.
Possible response: People are attracted to the variety of landforms and climates
in the Pacific states and to the many national parks and forests. California's
beaches, climate, movie studios, and amusement parks are popular tourist
attractions in the region. So are the mountains and rivers of the Pacific Northwest
and Alaska. Tourists are attracted to Hawaii for its island landscapes, Polynesian
culture, and attractions, such as Hawaii Volcanoes National Park.

88 ▪ Assessment Program   Chapter 12 Test

© Harcourt

ANSWERS

5 Test

Part One: Test Your Understanding

MULTIPLE CHOICE (2 points each)

Directions Circle the letter of the best answer.

1 Why are many peaks in the Rocky Mountains among the sharpest and highest in North America?
A because the Rocky Mountains affect the flow of many rivers across the continent
B because more snow falls on the peaks of the Rockies than at lower elevations
C because erosion has not rounded or smoothed the peaks over time
D because the Rocky Mountains are the oldest mountain range on the continent

2 The Rocky Mountains were a great barrier to east-to-west travel in the United States until—
F the transcontinental railroad was built.
G Lewis and Clark explored the mountains.
H the first interstate highways were built.
J airplanes were invented.

3 Which of these statements about temperature and mountains is true?
A Mountain climates are always very cold.
B Temperatures go down as you go up a mountain.
C Warm temperatures stop trees from growing on mountains.
D Mountain climates are always dry.

4 Which of these national parks is the oldest in the United States?
F Grand Canyon National Park
G Hawaii Volcanoes National Park
H Yellowstone National Park
J Petrified Forest National Park

5 What did the Hohokam and Anasazi Indians do that enabled them to live in one place?
A They started using horses to hunt buffalo.
B They won wars against their neighbors.
C They discovered how to use adobe to build houses.
D They developed irrigation systems to grow food.

6 Why do many people in the West region celebrate both Mexican and United States holidays?
F Many families in the region trace their roots to Mexico.
G People from Mexico were the first to live in the region.
H Mexico was once part of the United States.
J Both countries share the common border of the Rio Grande.

7 What effect do mountains have on the deserts in the West region?
A The mountains prevent travel across the deserts.
B When the mountain snows melt, they bring droughts to the deserts.
C The mountains stop winds from creating sand dunes.
D The mountains keep moist air from reaching the deserts.

8 What can cause a flood in the desert?
F a cloudburst
G a tornado
H an arroyo
J a drought

9 The climate of the Pacific Northwest is especially good for growing—
A pineapples and coconuts.
B cotton and wheat.
C apples and pears.
D oranges and grapefruit.

10 What were the last two states to join the United States?
F Arizona and Nevada
G Alaska and Hawaii
H Oregon and Washington
J Idaho and Montana

11 The nation's leading manufacturing state is—
A Washington.
B Arizona.
C California.
D Colorado.

12 Which of the following is *not* an industry in Hawaii?
F banking
G food processing
H oil refining
J tourism

(continued)

MULTIPLE CHOICE (2 points each)

Directions For each group of terms, circle the letter of the term that does *not* belong with the other two.

13 a. Ring of Fire   b. Pacific Rim   **c.** Death Valley

14 **a.** fjord   b. mesa   c. butte

15 a. mission   **b.** oil slick   c. society

16 **a.** reservation   b. forty-niner   c. boomtown

17 a. sand dune   b. oasis   **c.** terrace

18 a. satellite   b. telegraph   **c.** geyser

19 a. rain shadow   **b.** migrant worker   c. barrier

SHORT ANSWER (2 points each)

Directions Write the answer to each question on the lines provided.

20 Where do most people in the western mountain regions live?

in cities located in valleys between the mountains, or in cities located on plains or plateaus east or west of the mountains

21 Why is water conservation especially important in the West region?

because much of the region is dry, desert land, where natural sources of fresh water are scarce; because the population is growing faster than natural sources of fresh water can be replaced

22 How did mining affect the West region?

It attracted many people to move to the region; cities often grew up near the mines.

23 How did the completion of the transcontinental railroad affect the West region?

It allowed faster travel and communication between the West region and the rest of the country, bringing more settlers to the region.

(continued)

Part Two: Test Your Skills

READ A TIME ZONE MAP (3 points each)

Directions Use the time zone map below to answer the questions that follow.

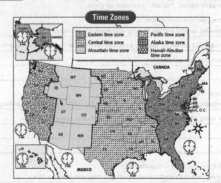

Time Zones

24 How many time zones are in the United States? six

25 In which time zone is the capital of the United States located? eastern time zone

26 When it is 11:00 A.M. in Utah, what time is it in Iowa? 12:00 P.M., or noon

27 When it is 1:00 P.M. in Missouri, what time is it in California? 11:00 A.M.

28 If you are in Nevada and you want to call a friend in Ohio when it is 9:30 P.M. there, what time should you make the call? 6:30 P.M.

(continued)

© Harcourt

ANSWERS

Name _____ Date _____

Part Three: Apply What You Have Learned

Directions Complete each of the following activities.

㉙ **IDENTIFY WESTERN LOCATIONS ON A MAP** (19 points)

Match each description below with the correct number on the map on page 94.
Write the number from the map in the space provided.

a. __2__ the wettest place in the United States

b. __6__ the city built to be the capital of Spanish New Mexico

c. __4__ one of the only places in the United States with rain forests

d. __3__ the lowest and driest place in the United States

e. __1__ the highest mountain in the United States

f. __8__ the place where the Anasazi settled

g. __7__ the dam that created Lake Mead, one of the world's largest reservoirs

h. __5__ the highest capital city in the United States

On the map on page 94, use a different color to shade each of the three regions of the West—the Mountain states, the Southwest Desert states, and the Pacific states. Then, in the chart below, fill in the names of the states that make up each region.

Mountain States	Southwest Desert States	Pacific States
Colorado	Arizona	Alaska
Idaho	Nevada	California
Montana	New Mexico	Hawaii
Utah		Oregon
Wyoming		Washington

Students should shade each of the three West regions a different color on the map.

(continued)

Unit 5 Test   Assessment Program ▪ 93

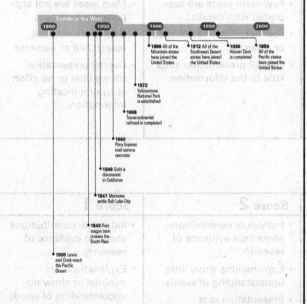

94 ▪ Assessment Program   Unit 5 Test

Name _____ Date _____

㉚ **USE A TIME LINE** (10 points)

The time line below shows some important events that occurred in the West region during the past 200 years. Use the time line to answer the questions on page 96.

Events in the West

1800 — 1850 — 1900 — 1950 — 2000

- 1896 All of the Mountain states have joined the United States
- 1912 All of the Southwest Desert states have joined the United States
- 1936 Hoover Dam is completed
- 1959 All of the Pacific states have joined the United States
- 1872 Yellowstone National Park is established
- 1869 Transcontinental railroad is completed
- 1860 Pony Express mail service operates
- 1848 Gold is discovered in California
- 1847 Mormons settle Salt Lake City
- 1843 First wagon train crosses the South Pass
- 1805 Lewis and Clark reach the Pacific Ocean

Unit 5 Test   Assessment Program ▪ 95

Name _____ Date _____

a. When was Yellowstone National Park established?

1872

b. Which two events on the time line occurred within ___ year of each other?

The Mormons settled Salt Lake City, and gold wa___ covered in California.

c. By what year had all of the Southwest Desert st___ joined the United States?

1912

d. Which was completed first, Hoover Dam or ___ transcontinental railroad?

the transcontinental railroad

e. Why is the year 1843 important in the h___ry of the West region?

In this year the first wagon train cross___ the South Pass; the South Pass

opened the West region to settlers ___ the East.

㉛ **ESSAY** (10 points)

In a one-paragraph essay, explain ___ you think people have grouped the West states into the three regions used ___ our textbook.

Possible response: Like most o___ regions, people divide the West region into

smaller regions in order to st___ and compare the regions more easily. The

states that make up the We___ grouped into three regions based on shared

locations and physical fea___s. As their names suggest, the Mountain states

share the common feat___ of mountains; the Southwest Desert states share the

common feature of d___s; and the Pacific states share the common feature of

the Pacific coastlin___

96 ▪ Assessment Program   Unit 5 Test

ANSWER KEY   **Assessment Program** ▪ **143**

ANSWERS

Name _____ Date _____

Individual Performance Task

Western Environments

People throughout time have adapted to their different environments. In this task, you will write a short report on the ways in which a group of people adapted to their environment.

① Select one of the following environments to analyze. Then select one of the groups that lives or lived in that environment to be the subject of your report.

DESERTS	MOUNTAINS	COASTS AND ISLANDS
Hohokam and Anasazi Indians	Sherpas	Nez Perce and Chinook Indians
Israelis	Quechuas	Hawaiians

② Use your textbook, the Internet, or library resources to find out how your group adapted to the environment in which it lives or lived. Some of the things to consider are housing, farming, raising animals, industries, clothing, transportation, and culture.

③ Write a rough draft of your report. Have a classmate read it. Ask whether anything in the report is confusing.

④ Make a final copy of your report. Include with your final copy a map showing where your group lives or lived. You may also want to include pictures from magazines or newspapers, or draw your own pictures.

⑤ Share your report with your classmates.

Name _____ Date _____

Group Performance Task

West Words

A *lexicon* is a collection of words. In this task, your small group will create a book called *A Lexicon of the West*.

① With your group, brainstorm words from this unit, from A to Z, that deal with the West region of the United States. The words should be about the region's geography, economy, culture, or attractions. For example, an A word might be *adobe*, and a B word might be *boomtown*. The letter does not have to be the first letter of the word. For example, an X word might be *Phoenix*. Try to come up with as many words for each letter as possible.

② As a group, choose one word for each letter of the alphabet. It should be one for which a picture could be drawn to show its meaning or importance.

③ Divide the letters of the alphabet among your group members. Each person should be responsible for about the same number of letters. Each student will create a page for the lexicon for each of his or her words. There should be three parts to each page.

➧ PART 1   At the top of the page will be a heading that gives the letter and the word, such as *A is for adobe* or *B is for boomtown*.

➧ PART 2   In the center of the page will be a drawing showing the meaning of the word. For example, *A is for adobe* could show a drawing of a pueblo.

➧ PART 3   At the bottom of the page will be a two-sentence explanation of the importance of the word. For example, you could write, "The Anasazi used adobe to build their homes in the Southwest Desert region. Today, many buildings in the region still use this style of architecture."

④ One student from the group should make a cover sheet for the lexicon. Another should make a Table of Contents. In the Table of Contents, there should be one line for each letter. It should state the name of the page, such as *A is for adobe*, and the name of the student responsible for the page. When the lexicon is finished, your group can display it for others to enjoy.

INDIVIDUAL PERFORMANCE TASK

Score 4	Score 3	Score 2	Score 1
• Main ideas are well supported with details. • Details are well researched and accurate. • Overall presentation is very creative and informative.	• Main ideas are supported with details. • Details are researched and accurate. • Overall presentation is creative and informative.	• Few main ideas are supported with details. • Few details are researched or accurate. • Overall presentation adds little to the information.	• Main ideas are not supported with details. • Details are not well researched or accurate. • Overall presentation shows little or no effort at communicating information.

GROUP PERFORMANCE TASK

Score 4	Score 3	Score 2	Score 1
• Individual contributions are well researched and illustrated. • Explanations are very detailed and accurate. • Presentation follows the guidelines and is very clear.	• Individual contributions are researched and illustrated. • Explanations are accurate. • Presentation follows the guidelines.	• Individual contributions show little evidence of research. • Explanations show little understanding of words. • Presentation is at times inconsistent with guidelines.	• Individual contributions show no evidence of research. • Explanations are minimal or show no understanding of words. • Presentation does not follow guidelines.

ANSWERS

13 Test

Name _____ Date _____

Part One: Test Your Understanding

MULTIPLE CHOICE (4 points each)

Directions Circle the letter of the best answer.

1. Which of the following is *not* one of the fastest-growing regions in the United States?
   A the Sun Belt
   B the Great Plains (circled)
   C the Pacific Coast
   D the Atlantic Coast

2. Which of the following statements explains why there are many different customs in the United States?
   F There are many factories in the United States.
   G The United States has a free enterprise economy.
   H People from many places brought their customs here. (circled)
   J As a country grows older, its people develop more customs.

3. Which of these do all people in the United States share?
   A the same customs
   B the same language
   C the same government and laws (circled)
   D the same foods and drinks

4. How do people in the United States remember their country's history?
   F by celebrating holidays and visiting monuments (circled)
   G by buying and selling goods and services
   H by voting in general elections
   J by volunteering in community organizations

5. In the United States, citizens do *not* have the right to—
   A make choices about what kind of work to do.
   B have a fair trial by jury.
   C make decisions that take away the rights of others. (circled)
   D say what they think about the government.

6. Which of the following is *not* a factor of production?
   F human resources
   G natural resources
   H capital resources
   J government resources (circled)

Chapter 13 Test

Assessment Program ■ 99

Name _____ Date _____

7. If the demand for a good or service is high and the supply is low,—
   A prices generally rise. (circled)
   B prices generally fall.
   C few people will want to buy it.
   D the company will produce less of it.

8. Why do economic experts often call the time in which we live the "Information Age"?
   F because the United States produces most of the movies in the world
   G because more information and technology is available today than ever before (circled)
   H because most Americans today work in high-tech industries
   J because the United States takes part in the global economy

MATCHING (4 points each)

Directions Match each term on the right with its meaning. Then write the correct letter in the space provided.

	Meaning	Term
9. C	an unfair feeling of dislike or hatred for a group of people because of their background, race, or religion	A. monument
10. F	a saying chosen to express the ideals of a nation, state, or group	B. democracy
11. A	something that is built to remind people of the past	C. prejudice
12. B	a form of government in which the people rule by making decisions themselves or by electing leaders to make decisions for them	D. interest
13. E	a way of deciding something by voting	E. majority rule
14. G	the money a business earns after everything is paid for	F. motto
15. D	the money a bank or borrower pays for the use of money	G. profit

100 ■ Assessment Program

Chapter 13 Test

Name _____ Date _____

Part Two: Test Your Skills

DETERMINE POINTS OF VIEW (4 points each)

Directions Each of the state mottoes below was chosen to represent that state's ideals, people, geography, or history. Write a sentence or two explaining the point of view you think each state motto expresses.

16. ALASKA: "North to the Future"
   Possible response: Alaska is the northernmost state and was one of the last states to join the Union. Its motto encourages people to move there.

17. INDIANA: "The Crossroads of America"
   Possible response: Indiana is located close to the center of the United States; its location makes it a crossroads of different regions in the country.

18. KENTUCKY: "United We Stand, Divided We Fall"
   Possible response: To succeed, people must work together; otherwise, they may fail. Some students may say that the motto refers to the Civil War and Kentucky's role as a border state during the conflict.

19. MASSACHUSETTS: "By the Sword We Seek Peace, but Peace Only Under Liberty" Possible response: Massachusetts was the site of the first battle of the American Revolution. The motto expresses the view that Americans are willing to fight if necessary to protect their freedoms and liberties.

20. MICHIGAN: "If You Seek a Pleasant Peninsula, Look Around You"
   Possible response: Michigan is made up of two peninsulas; it invites residents and guests to appreciate the pleasantness of life there.

(continued)

Chapter 13 Test

Assessment Program ■ 101

Name _____ Date _____

Part Three: Apply What You Have Learned

Directions Complete each of the following activities.

21. IDENTIFY CAUSE AND EFFECT (10 points)
   Fill in the missing cause or effect to complete the chart below. Possible answers are written in the chart.

CAUSE	→	EFFECT
People in other countries sometimes face poverty and prejudice.	→	People from other countries have left their homelands and immigrated to the United States.
People from other cultures have brought different kinds of foods to the United States.	→	People in the United States eat oranges, apples, spaghetti, tacos, and egg rolls.
People in the United States volunteer to share responsibilities for the well-being of their communities.	→	By working together, Americans can share ideas and help solve problems.
The United States government makes and carries out laws.	→	People in the United States can live together in order and safety.
The United States takes part in the global economy.	→	The United States' economy is interdependent with economies around the world.

22. ESSAY (10 points)
   When President John F. Kennedy was a young man, he wrote a book about the United States. He called the book *A Nation of Immigrants*. In a one-paragraph essay, explain why this is a good title for a book about the history of the United States.
   Possible response: Whether they came willingly, as most Europeans, Asians, and Hispanics did, or unwillingly, as most Africans did, almost everyone in the United States has ancestors from another country. Therefore, most Americans either are immigrants or are descended from immigrants, making the United States a nation of immigrants.

102 ■ Assessment Program

Chapter 13 Test

© Harcourt

ANSWERS

14 Test

Name _____ Date _____

Part One: Test Your Understanding

MULTIPLE CHOICE (4 points each)

Directions Circle the letter of the best answer.

❶ Which of the following is *not* a purpose of the United States Constitution?
A to explain how our federal government works
B to unite the 50 states under one federal government
C to describe the rights that people in the United States have
(D) to organize the economy of the United States

❷ In which branch of the federal government do senators work?
F the executive branch
G the military branch
(H) the legislative branch
J the judicial branch

❸ How can the judicial branch of the federal government check the power of the legislative branch?
(A) by ruling that a law does not follow the Constitution
B by overriding a President's veto
C by rejecting a person chosen for the Supreme Court
D by vetoing a law passed by Congress

❹ Which of the following is a responsibility of local governments?
F printing money
G delivering the mail
H building railroads
(J) collecting garbage

❺ Why do all levels of government collect taxes?
A to conduct elections
B to ensure equal rights for all citizens
(C) to pay for the services they provide
D to pay for political campaigns

❻ Which of the following rights is *not* guaranteed by the First Amendment to the United States Constitution?
F freedom of religion
(G) the right to vote in a general election
H freedom of speech
J the right to hold meetings to discuss problems and share information

❼ Why does the United States form alliances with other countries?
A to conquer these countries
B to make sure everyone in the world follows the same religion
(C) to maintain peaceful relations around the world
D because it is required by the United Nations

CATEGORIZE (4 points each)

Directions Read each description below. If it describes the federal government, write *F* in the space. If it describes state governments, write *S* in the space. If the statement describes both levels of government, write *B* in the space.

❽ __B__ It collects taxes from citizens to pay for services.

❾ __F__ It prints and coins money in the United States.

❿ __S__ It oversees state colleges and state universities.

⓫ __B__ It sets up court systems.

⓬ __F__ It oversees trade with other countries.

⓭ __B__ It provides for the public health and welfare.

⓮ __S__ It sets up public schools.

⓯ __F__ It declares war and makes peace.

(continued)

Chapter 14 Test   Assessment Program ▪ 103

104 ▪ Assessment Program   Chapter 14 Test

Name _____ Date _____

Part Two: Test Your Skills

READ A FLOW CHART (2 points each)

Directions To make a law, state governments follow a process that is nearly identical to the process that the federal government follows. Fill in the missing information in this flow chart to explain how a bill becomes a law in the state governments.

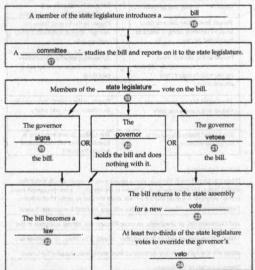

HOW A BILL BECOMES A STATE LAW

A member of the state legislature introduces a __bill__ .
⑯

A __committee__ studies the bill and reports on it to the state legislature.
⑰

Members of the __state legislature__ vote on the bill.
⑱

The governor __signs__ ⑲ the bill.
OR
The governor __holds the bill and does nothing with it.__ ⑳
OR
The governor __vetoes__ ㉑ the bill.

The bill becomes a __law__ ㉒

The bill returns to the state assembly for a new __vote__ ㉓

At least two-thirds of the state legislature votes to override the governor's __veto__ ㉔.

(continued)

Chapter 14 Test   Assessment Program ▪ 105

Name _____ Date _____

Part Three: Apply What You Have Learned

Directions Complete each of the following activities.

㉕ COMPARE THE BRANCHES OF THE FEDERAL GOVERNMENT (12 points)

In the chart below, each box stands for a branch of the federal government.

Fill in the names of the three branches and the main job of each branch.

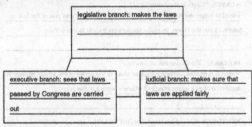

legislative branch: makes the laws

executive branch: sees that laws passed by Congress are carried out

judicial branch: makes sure that laws are applied fairly

㉖ ESSAY (10 points)

In 1863 President Abraham Lincoln gave a speech that came to be called the Gettysburg Address. Read the following excerpt from that speech. Then write a one-paragraph essay explaining what you think Lincoln was trying to express.

"...our fathers brought forth on this continent, a new nation, conceived in Liberty, and dedicated to the proposition that all men are created equal.... we here highly resolve ... that government of the people, by the people, for the people, shall not perish from the earth."

Possible response: Abraham Lincoln was reminding the audience that the United States of America was formed by the people to ensure equal rights, opportunities, and representation for the people. Lincoln was asking the audience to remember the ideas of liberty on which the country's history is based. Citizens today have a responsibility to see that freedom and liberty are preserved for future generations.

106 ▪ Assessment Program   Chapter 14 Test

© Harcourt

ANSWERS

Name _____ Date _____

6 Test

Part One: Test Your Understanding

MULTIPLE CHOICE (2 points each)

Directions Circle the letter of the best answer.

1 Why do some people call the United States a "nation of immigrants"?
A The country has many visitors from around the world.
B Most people in the United States are not citizens.
C People from around the world have come here to live.
D The country's economy is based on world trade.

2 Which of the following foods eaten in the United States did *not* come from other places?
F corn
G oranges
H pasta
J apples

3 What is the motto of the United States?
A We the People
B Out of Many, One
C All for One, and One for All
D Government of the People

4 Saluting the American flag during a parade expresses—
F patriotism.
G prejudice.
H majority rule.
J free enterprise.

5 Why is July 4 an important day for all Americans?
A On that day, the American Civil War ended.
B On that day, the United States declared independence from Britain.
C On that day, the Pilgrims arrived in present-day Massachusetts.
D On that day, representatives signed the United States Constitution.

6 In a democracy the people—
F make choices about the government by voting.
G are not represented in the government.
H have few responsibilities.
J have fewer rights than the leaders of the government.

(continued)

Unit 6 Test   Assessment Program ■ 107

Name _____ Date _____

7 Which of the following is *not* a responsibility of citizenship?
A voting in elections
B obeying traffic signals
C running campaigns
D paying taxes

8 What do retail trade industries do?
F loan, handle, and collect money
G buy goods and sell them directly to consumers
H produce and use information-processing software and hardware
J buy large amounts of goods from producers and sell them to other businesses

9 What do most business owners consider when they decide what goods to produce or services to offer, and how much to charge for them?
A supply and demand
B the global economy
C factors of production
D interest on loans

10 What keeps any one branch of the government from becoming too powerful?
F supply and demand
G checks and balances
H taxes and budgets
J imports and exports

11 Which of these is a responsibility of the federal government?
A fixing streetlights
B selling farm products
C running the army
D collecting garbage

12 Which of these is a responsibility of a state government?
F setting up public schools
G buying fire trucks
H delivering the mail
J cleaning city streets

13 Which of the following is *not* a way that the Civil Rights movement worked to meet its goals?
A holding demonstrations
B organizing marches
C not voting in elections
D not buying certain products

(continued)

108 ■ Assessment Program   Unit 6 Test

Name _____ Date _____

14 MATCHING (1 point each)

Directions Match the terms on the left with the meanings on the right. Then, in the boxes on page 110, write each number next to the correct letter. You can check your work by adding the numbers in each row or column. You should get the same number as a sum no matter which row or column of numbers you add. Find this magic number.

Term	Meaning
a. immigrant	1. the document that gives the plan for the federal government
b. civil rights	2. the branch of the federal government that sees that the laws are carried out fairly
c. judicial branch	3. the condition of being poor
d. poverty	4. something that is built to remind people of the past
e. alliance	5. the head of the executive branch in state governments
f. governor	6. a signed request for action
g. county	7. the branch of government that makes the laws
h. capital resources	8. a partnership between countries or groups of people
i. majority rule	9. a form of government in which the people rule by making decisions themselves or by electing leaders to make decisions for them
j. democracy	10. the money, buildings, machines, and tools needed to run a business
k. legislative branch	11. the level of government for which a sheriff works
l. petition	12. a way of deciding something by voting
m. Constitution	13. a person who comes to live in a country from some other place
n. monument	14. a plan for spending money
o. budget	15. the branch of government that sees that laws that are passed are carried out
p. executive branch	16. the rights of citizens to equal treatment under the law

(continued)

Unit 6 Test   Assessment Program ■ 109

Name _____ Date _____

Magic Number = __34__

a. = 13	b. = 16	c. = 2	d. = 3
e. = 8	f. = 5	g. = 11	h. = 10
i. = 12	j. = 9	k. = 7	l. = 6
m. = 1	n. = 4	o. = 14	p. = 15

SHORT ANSWER (2 points each)

Directions Write the answer to each question on the lines provided.

15 Name two things that all people in the United States share and that help unite them all. Possible responses: a way of life; their country's history and its holidays; a belief in freedom; a national government; rights and responsibilities

16 How does the United States economy offer Americans choices?
Possible responses: Americans are free to start and run businesses with little interference from the government; people can work at many different kinds of jobs; consumers can choose from many different products and services.

17 Why did early leaders of the United States add the Bill of Rights to the Constitution? Possible responses: to protect people's rights; to make official the freedoms that the government cannot take away and the actions that the government is not allowed to take

18 Why does the United States play a special role among the countries of the world? because the United States is a wealthy, powerful, and democratic nation

(continued)

110 ■ Assessment Program   Unit 6 Test

ANSWER KEY

Assessment Program ■ 147

ANSWERS

Name _____ Date _____

Part Two: Test Your Skills
READ A POPULATION MAP (3 points each)

Directions Use the information in the population map on page 112 to answer the questions below.

19 Which part of the United States has a higher population density, the Atlantic Coast or the Pacific Coast? Atlantic Coast

20 In general, which country has a higher population density, Canada or the United States? United States

21 What is the population density in and around Mexico City, Mexico?
125–250 and 60–125 people per square mile

22 Why do you think the area closest to the United States border has the highest population density in Canada? Possible response: Because much of northern Canada has an extremely cold climate.

23 Which part of Texas has a greater population density, the eastern half or the western half? Why do you think the population in Texas is spread out that way? the eastern half; possible response: Because western Texas is mountainous and has a desert or arid climate.

24 Which city probably has more factories, Anchorage, Alaska, or Los Angeles, California? Explain your answer. Los Angeles, California; possible response: Because Los Angeles is a larger city with a higher population density, there are probably more factories for people to work in.

(continued)

Unit 6 Test   Assessment Program ■ 111

Name _____ Date _____

Population of North America

(continued)

112 ■ Assessment Program   Unit 6 Test

Name _____ Date _____

Part Three: Apply What You Have Learned

Directions Complete each of the following activities.

25 ANALYZE NATIONAL SYMBOLS (6 points)
Below are three symbols of our nation's heritage, history, and government. Explain what each symbol stands for. Possible responses are given.

The Presidential Seal shows that the United States is an independent, united country. It represents the country's strength and love of peace and freedom.

The Liberty Bell stands for the freedom that the people in the United States have fought for over the years.

The Statue of Liberty stands for the freedom and the many opportunities that the United States has always offered to immigrants over the years.

(continued)

Unit 6 Test   Assessment Program ■ 113

Name _____ Date _____

26 TRUE OR FALSE (2 points each)
Read each sentence below. Write T in the space next to the sentence if it is true and F if the sentence is false. If the sentence is false, cross out the word that makes it false and, above that word, write the correct word to make it true.

a. __T__ In the past, most immigrants to the United States came from Europe.
b. __F__ The United States government is a monarchy. [democracy]
c. __T__ The governor heads the executive branch of state government.
d. __F__ Many immigrants came to the United States to escape wealth. [poverty]
e. __F__ State governments manage public utilities, such as water and electricity. [Local]
f. __T__ When you vote on which game to play, you are using majority rule.
g. __F__ During an election, most candidates carry on a petition. [campaign]
h. __F__ The United States takes part in the local economy by trading goods and services with other countries. [global]

27 ESSAY (10 points)
In a one-paragraph essay, describe how you think that your rights as a citizen of the United States relate to your responsibilities as a citizen.
Possible response: Citizens in the United States have many rights, but with those rights come many responsibilities. For example, with the right to elect government leaders comes the responsibility of learning about issues and voting. With the right to a fair trial comes the responsibility of serving on juries. Because all citizens have freedom of speech and religion, they also have the responsibility to respect those same rights for others. With having the right to make and change laws, all citizens also have the responsibility to obey those laws. Finally, because Americans have fought to win these rights for all Americans, citizens today have the responsibility to protect those rights for future generations.

114 ■ Assessment Program   Unit 6 Test

---

148 ■ Assessment Program   **ANSWER KEY**

ANSWERS

Name _____ Date _____

Individual Performance Task

Immigrant Stories

As you know, immigrants from all over the world have been coming to the United States for centuries. They have come in search of a new life in a new place with new opportunities. In this task, you will create the diary of a young immigrant who has come to America with his or her family.

❶ Select one of the following stories as the basis for your diary:

- an immigrant coming to the American colonies for religious freedom
- an immigrant coming to the United States in the late 1800s or early 1900s to escape poverty
- an immigrant coming to the United States today to escape wars in his or her homeland

❷ Use a blank outline map of the world to show the country from which you have come, where in the United States you have settled, and the route you took to get to the United States.

❸ Use your textbook, library resources, and the Internet to research the country from which you came and the region of the United States where you have settled.

❹ Write at least five diary entries for different events that occurred during your immigration to the United States. One of the entries should explain why you left your home country. Another entry should tell about an experience you had on your journey and describe the mode of transportation you used. A third entry should describe how you felt when you reached your new home. The remaining entries should tell about events and experiences of your daily life as a newly arrived immigrant in the United States. Be creative, but be historically accurate as well.

❺ Use pictures from newspapers or magazines to illustrate some of your diary entries, or draw your own pictures. Write a caption for each picture to describe what it shows and to identify which diary entry it is illustrating.

❻ Make a cover for your diary, and share your diary with your classmates.

Unit 6 Test   Assessment Program ▪ 115

Name _____ Date _____

Group Performance Task

City Council Election

The city council is an important part of local government. It makes the laws for its city, just as state legislatures and Congress make the laws for states and the nation. In this task, your class will hold a mock election for members of your city council.

❶ **Select Candidates** In this election, six members will be elected to the city council. Form groups of three students each. One student in each group will be the candidate for city council, one will be the campaign manager, and one will be the campaign worker.

❷ **Select Issues** As a class, choose five major issues in your community to be the platform of the campaign. Perhaps you can invite a member of your city council to speak to the class about some of the major issues in your community. Newspapers and your local library are sources where you can get information about local issues.

❸ **Organize a Campaign** Decide among your group what position your candidate will take on each issue. Make up campaign posters to tell people about your candidate. You may wish to use a catchy slogan, or saying, on the posters. The campaign manager and worker should make flyers that tell what the candidate believes. They should hand out the flyers to other students.

❹ **Give Campaign Speeches** Each campaign manager will give a one-minute speech introducing the candidate to the class. Each candidate will then give a two-minute speech to the class, explaining his or her ideas and positions on the issues.

❺ **Go to the Polls** Using a secret ballot, each student—including the candidates—should vote for six members of the city council. Announce the results of the election. Then discuss how individual campaigns might have led to the success of certain candidates.

116 ▪ Assessment Program   Unit 6 Test

INDIVIDUAL PERFORMANCE TASK

Score 4	Score 3	Score 2	Score 1
• Description is rich and vivid. • Details are historically very accurate. • Character is well developed. • Diary entries are well organized and presented.	• Description is lively. • Details are in general historically accurate. • Character is reasonably developed. • Diary entries are reasonably well organized and presented.	• Little description is given. • Details are historically not very accurate. • Character is minimally developed. • Diary entries are poorly organized and presented.	• No description is provided. • The few details are not historically accurate. • Character is not developed. • Diary entries are not organized and are poorly presented.

GROUP PERFORMANCE TASK

Score 4	Score 3	Score 2	Score 1
• Individual involvement shows deep understanding of the issues. • The process evolves through detailed discussion, research, and cooperation. • Presentations are very effective.	• Individual involvement shows understanding of the issues. • The process evolves through reasonable discussion, research, and cooperation. • Presentations are effective.	• Individual involvement shows little understanding of the issues. • The process occurs with little discussion, research, or cooperation. • Presentations are of limited effectiveness.	• Individual involvement shows no understanding of the issues. • The process reflects no real discussion, research, or cooperation. • Presentations are not effective.

Individual Performance Task

Immigrant Stories

Group Performance Task

City Council Election

INDIVIDUAL PERFORMANCE TASK

Score 4	Score 3	Score 2	Score 1
• Description is rich and vivid.	• Description is lively.	• Little description is given.	• No description is provided.
• Details are historically very accurate.	• Details are in general historically accurate.	• Details are historically not very accurate.	• The few details are not historically accurate.
• Character is well developed.	• Character is reasonably developed.	• Character is minimally developed.	• Character is not developed.
• Diary entries are well organized and presented.	• Diary entries are reasonably well organized and presented.	• Diary entries are poorly organized and presented.	• Diary entries are not organized and are poorly presented.

GROUP PERFORMANCE TASK

Score 4	Score 3	Score 2	Score 1
• Individual involvement shows deep understanding of the issues.	• Individual involvement shows understanding of the issues.	• Individual involvement shows little understanding of the issues.	• Individual involvement shows no understanding of the issues.
• The process evolves through detailed discussion, research, and cooperation.	• The process evolves through reasonable discussion, research and cooperation.	• The process occurs with little discussion, research, or cooperation.	• The process reflects no real discussion, research, or cooperation.
• Presentations are very effective.	• Presentations are effective.	• Presentations are of limited effectiveness	• Presentations are not effective.